The Ridge

A Gemütlichkeit Community

The history of the Ridge is an account of hard-working German immigrants from Hanover, Germany as they stettled in Perry County, Missouri, in the 1850s. The Rauhs take the reader through this early German life in America.

These early folks were a part of a Gemütlichkeit community. They were an early community of closeness bound by a strong Christian fiath. Read on and learn about farm life in the early years in Perry County, Missouri.

Charles Rauh

Charles Rauh *in his retirement years has written several books. He is a retired health care executive, having spent his life managing hospitals and nursing homes. Charles is a graduate of St. Paul College in Concordia, Missouri. He divides his free time between teaching an adult Bible class, writing books, and fishing when he can. He serves as a docent at the Lutheran Heritage Center and Museum in Altenburg, Missouri. Charles and his wife Eileen live in Perryville, MO.*

Barbara Rauh *Powell lives in Pocahontas, Missouri. She is a graduate of Southeast Missouri State Univerisyt, and a post-graduate of the University of Missouri-Saint Louis. In Barbara's retirement, she has been helping Charles with his writing and volunteer work. She serves as a docent athe Lutheran Heritage Center & Museum in Altenburg, MO.*

ISBN 9781728836546

Acknowledgements

Much research was necessary to write this book. There were several people who assisted with research and they deserve to be mentioned. First is Barbara Rauh Powell. She not only encouraged me to write about the Ridge, she did extensive research for the writing. Barbara's work makes her deservedly co-author of this book.

Gerard Fiehler, Lynn Degenhardt, and Warren Schmidt provided valuable information in writing this history. These three are mainstays and Docents at the Lutheran Heritage Center and Museum in Altenburg, Missouri.

Linda Paulish, Mary Kiehne, Richard Weber, Eunice Schlichting and Leo Steffens each were willing to be interviewed about The Ridge. I thank this group.

Then there my cousins who willingly shared information. I must mention David Stueve and his wife, Debbie, Mary Rhodes, Nancy Monier, and Marcia Mendola. I thank you for your input.

We would like to specifically recognize brothers John, Herb, and Bob Rauh. These loved the Ridge and the Gemelnde, Kirche, Kamradschaft Arbeit and Gemütlichkeit found here. The boys died young and will always be missed.

Locations
on cover

1. Rudy Steffens
2. Star Landing
2A. Daniel Wiehern
3. Weber's Place
4. Ridge School
5. Martin Stueve
6. Ernot (Fish) Stueve
7. Rudy Stueve
8. Dick Miesner
9. Herb Doering
10. Ernst Doering
11. Brauner Bros
12. Ed Leimbach
13. Theo Holschen
14. Leo Steffens
15. Seventy-Six Town
16. Mack's Chapel
17. Wilkenson
18. G Thurm
19. J Holschen
20. Neunert/Jacob, IL
21. Albert Leimbach

Table of Contents

INTRODUCTION

This book is about a small community of German Saxons that emerged in the late 1800's called the Ridge, which is about six miles north of Altenburg, Missouri. The Ridge is an appropriate description for this area of Perry County, Missouri. Traveling north from Altenburg one descends a steep hill and at the bottom the road is straight up to the Ridge. One is truly on top of the ridge when you arrive. This east-west terrain stretches from the Wittenberg, Missouri bottoms for about six miles to the west. The Ridge follows the Mississippi River which runs east-west on its journey to the Gulf of Mexico.

In this area of The Ridge there is a second ridge. It stands just as high as the first ridge. However, its east-west length is much shorter than the first ridge. From atop the second ridge one has a beautiful view of the Illinois bottoms, the Mississippi River, and the towns of Neunert and Jacob, Illinois.

As history evolved the Ridge became a small community of farmers that had its beginning shortly after 1839. The Ridge was never a town in Perry County. However, in the eastern part of Perry County if one referred to the Ridge everyone knew where it was.

The Ridge had its beginning at the time of a massive exodus of Europeans from that continent to the United States. The Industrial Revolution was begun and people were out of work. Manpower had been replaced by machine power and steam power. There was no work to be found. Germans were looking at the United States as an alternative to life in their country.

There were "push" and "pull" factors that influenced the migration of Germans to the United States. The first of the push reasons for leaving was service in the military. Wars and invasions were a common occurrence in Germany. Men were forced to serve to protect the homeland or to invade a neighboring country. As a result, men fled Germany to avoid service in the military. The threat of war was a cause of leaving Germany for many decades.

Another push factor was the drought of 1836-1840. There was little rain and the harvest was meager, wheat crops failed and there was a potato blight. This added to the misery.
The wine crop failed and all that was left was to take bad potatoes and distill potato whiskey. Along the Elbe River many farms were lost during this period.

In 1821 there were no Germans living in St. Louis. By 1824 there were a dozen Germans in St. Louis. In 1832 there were less than thirty Germans in St. Louis. Then the floodgates of German immigration opened. From 1839 to 1847 they poured into St. Louis by the thousands. In 1839 there were 68,069 immigrants who came to the United States. Of these 21, 028 were Germans. Of the entire total 10,306 arrived in New Orleans. Of these immigrants 2,691 came from Germany. One third of this number eventually came to Perry County.

The single and greatest reason for the German emigration which began in the 1830's was the Industrial Revolution. Goods were no longer processed one at a time but on an assembly line. The economy and job market were turned upside down. Cities began to grow. No longer did one produce linen on antiquated looms in the home. What set in was what we call today a recession. It was the economy that pushed Germans out of Europe and into the United States.

The pull factors: It was said that in St. Louis, the city was growing so fast that everyone had a job. If you wanted to farm the word was that land was cheap and there was plenty. There was timber aplenty to build homes. Anyone who could swing and ax and plow a furrow couldn't miss.

Another pull factor: We will not be alone. There are many from Saxony already living in America. We will associate with people that speak German and worship like we do now. These Germans saw this as a "can't miss" opportunity.

Saxons were indeed pushed and pulled as they considered emigrating. When they boarded ships for the journey across the Atlantic Ocean one wishes he could have heard the conversations among the people. How large will my farm be? Is there a church where I can worship? What are the laws in America? Are you allowed to speak German? and on and on. Sure, wish I was there to hear the conversations.

The folks that settled the Altenburg and Frohna area were predominately from Dresden, Saxony. These Ridge folks were from the Hanover region. Germans were streaming into the United States in large numbers. It is little wonder that these Hanoverians came to the Perry County area. They would have known that other German immigrants were living in this area. They also knew there was available land to be purchased and at reasonable and affordable prices.

Early on this community of Saxons named their area of settlement Friedland. This is translated into the English as Land of Peace. For these early settlers, Friedland was an appropriate name. Life in Germany was anything but peaceful.

The Ridge settlers no doubt knew of the Saxon settlements at Wittenberg, Altenburg, and Frohna. Most came to New Orleans and then boarded a steamboat for the trip north. These Hanoverians were not accompanied by clergy. These immigrants had no gesellschaft or association as did the Altenburg folks nor did they have a common treasury. Each family was on its own.

It needs to be noted that The Ridge people never established a church in this area called Friedland. This does not mean that they did not worship. Throughout the history of The Ridge there was a close tie between The Ridge and Immanuel Lutheran Church in Altenburg. The folks settling this area saw a need for a school. It was Immanuel Church that made possible a school on the Ridge. This certainly would explain the tie between these Ridge folks and Immanuel Church. It is known that during the winter months when the temperature was freezing and the snow deep, the Pastor at Immanuel Church conducted worship services in The Ridge school. The area residents called this the Friedland Geminde or Friedland Congregation.

Before the reader of this history can begin a study that person needs to become familiar with a particular vocabulary of the English language which is spoken in East Perry County Missouri. This vocabulary has to do with the power of prepositions. When you travel in Perry County, one needs to describe the destination by properly using the correct preposition.

A person living in Farrar wanting to go to Frohna knows that he will travel down to Frohna. A person in Frohna wishing to go to Farrar would describe the trip as back to Farrar. If you live in Longtown or even Perryville, the trip to Farrar is back.

If you live in Frohna and wish to go to Altenburg, you go over to Altenburg. Likewise, if you travel from Altenburg to Frohna, you go over to Frohna. Always remember that both of these towns go back to Farrar.

Should Frohna, Altenburg, or Farrar wish to go to Wittenberg, the direction of travel is down to Wittenberg. If you live in Wittenberg it gets somewhat complicated. From Wittenberg, one goes up to Altenburg and then over or out to Frohna. Never forget that all go back to Farrar.

Everyone in the area knows that the trip to New Wells, Pocahontas, Jackson and "the Cape" is a trip down. One travels up to Perryville and down to "the Cape".

Never ever forget, it is back to Farrar. Also, don't forget that to go to Uniontown is to go out to Uniontown.

We now come to The Ridge. How does one describe the destination of the Ridge? The Ridge is a high topographical location. The road to The Ridge is straight up at the end. Yet you do not go up to The Ridge, you go back to The Ridge. No matter from what direction one is traveling, it is back.

If one in conversation said he was going over to the Ridge, or over to Farrar we would get questioning glances. That is not a proper way to describe your destination. Nor should anyone say he is going up to the Ridge. You just can't travel that direction. Ridge folks know that the direction to Wittenberg is down and a trip to Altenburg is up or out (it is never down or over).

One lives on the Ridge never at the Ridge. It is proper for these people to say they live back at the Ridge. These people never say they live up on the Ridge.

The reader is now prepared to read the history of the Ridge. The purpose of this book is to write a history of these hearty folks that left Germany in search of a better life. They began settling the Ridge about ten years after the 1839 Saxons established middle Perry County. One suspects the early Friedland people had an easier time of it than did the Altenburg and surrounding hamlets. They were not hindered or misled by clergy. They did not spend their first winter without shelter. They were able to do first things first.

There was in this region of Perry County two very distinct types of farming. In Wittenberg there were those who farmed the "bottoms." The land was flat and the soil some of the richest in the world. The major difficulty for these farmers was occasional flooding by the Mississippi River. The folks on The Ridge were "hill-farmers". The cleared fields were anything but flat. This presented a different type of farming. The early Ridge pioneers soon mastered the art of "hill-farming."

The history of the Ridge is a fascinating history. In this book we shall tell the story of farming as it once was. We shall relate faith, perseverance, and determination.

These were a different sort of folk. The Ridge was never an

incorporated town. The focal point of the community was Edmund Weber's store and tavern and the school. What united these people was their faith and their language. If someone in the community was hurt or needed help, the people responded. They would always come to the aid of each other. It would be several decades before they began to speak English.

This history of the Ridge will span many activities of life. We will visit threshing rings, hog butchering, education, church life, shipping goods, and of course, listening in on the telephone.

Prologue
Why write a book about the Ridge?

Now that's a good question. I thought that when my sister Barbara asked me to consider writing such a book. I was very familiar about the location of The Ridge, but is there a story about The Ridge? After one writes and describes the physical location and a topographical description, where does one look for the story about The Ridge?

I think I have found the story. It is in the location and in the topographics that the story is found. It is in the isolation and hills of The Ridge that one finds the story of pioneering, faith, and friendship. This story tells of the hardships the early settlers faced. Amid isolation from other early settlers The Ridge folks hacked out an early existence. On the sides of the hills they planted their crops and grazed their cattle. It is here the story is found.

The first question I had and wanted to explore is to find out about the first day of life on The Ridge. I tried to put myself in the early history and determine what my concerns would have been. It was soon apparent that food and shelter were paramount.

The first need of these German immigrants was a house and food for the family. That is where this book begins. They did not engage a real estate agent and select a farm with a house, barn, silo, grain bins, machine shed, and on and on. When they came into the area of the Ridge they found trees, trees, trees, hills, hills, and hills. That is how and where they began.

They constructed a simple home and early, very early, food was berries, squirrels, rabbits, turkey, deer and other game. After awhile came the rest of the food chain such as gardens, hogs, and sausage were a mainstay in their diet. Soon came a surplus of hogs. Now they have to butcher and cure hams. They made apple butter and molasses. Early on they mastered canning.

Progress was slow. There was little farming equipment. Again, let us be ridiculous to make a point. These early Ridge folks did not have $650,000 corn pickers and combines. Nor did they have eighteen row corn planters. The Ridge people threshed grain with a flail until the threshing machine was invented. They planted corn with a hoe putting two kernels into each hill.

They were always looking for a better way to get their jobs done. They hauled hay loose and put it into the barn. No hay bailers in those days. They milked their cows and sold the cream. You haven't lived until you have learned to milk and squirt milk into a kitten's mouth waiting for a drink.

It is in all this we find the story of The Ridge. These folks knew hard work and did their work without complaint. It is in the helping each other that The Ridge story exists. They worked hard for their own survival and helped their neighbor survive. The story of The Ridge hills and the people who make these hills their success form the story of the area. Perhaps area is the wrong word. It needs to be the community of people.

It is amazing to me that in the middle of the community of German immigrants their existed a community of back people. These people were left over families of former slaves. There was no animosity between black and white here. These black people were a community of people trying to survive just like the Germans were. I must say that the tolerance, patience, and support of the Steffens family stands out. They aided in the survival of both groups.

When I began my research on Ridge history I wondered if there would be people who would immerge and distinguish themselves among the Ridge people. I can tell you that there are people who stand out. At the end of this book I will name them.

The Ridge folks enjoyed a feeling of *Gemütlichkeit*. I will give you more later on a definition of that word. Because of their isolation from the rest of East Perry County they needed *Gemütlichkeit*. But there was something else. It was the Christian faith of the people. When the Ridge folks left Germany, they did not leave as the 1839 Saxons left. The 1839 Saxons were a group led by a leader. The Ridge folks came independently. They came primarily from Hanover Germany, in Saxony. There were Hanoverians that came to America as Lutherans and Lutherans they remained. They stayed in that faith and in spite of early problems they were a people who helped plant Lutheranism in America. The Ridge folks had a parochial school on the Ridge. They worshiped on the Ridge during inclement weather. With all the community they did not give up their faith.

I encourage you to read on and become acquainted with the folks on The Ridge. It is a history of hard work, faith, and perseverance. It is their unique history. It is a history to make us proud.

Chapter 1
COPING WITH ADVERSITY

The Ridge was settled mostly between 1850 and 1880. These immigrants had some education. They all had professions in Germany. A study of their German occupations reveals that many were cobblers, milliners (hat makers), linen weavers, and many other trades. The Industrial Revolution put the trades out of work and then came the recession. To emigrate and find a better life was their only way. There were only a few farmers who came to America. When they arrived, they found that the trades they knew were not needed. Just how many cobblers and linen weavers does The Ridge need? They became farmers of fields covered with trees. To farm the fields, they had to clear the land.

The Ridge people had reached a point of no return. They had no money to return, so, by necessity they had to adapt to the conditions and see if they could make a success out of life. Taylors and cabinet makers had to pick themselves up by the boot straps and begin a life of first surviving and then trying to be successful at farming,

The community of Altenburg had been settled for eleven years by 1850. They had been through the first phase, surviving. Many did not survive and hundreds died the first winter. There was some help in Altenburg for the folks back on The Ridge.

The first two needs to be addressed were shelter and food. A house came first and planting for food came immediately thereafter. The trees for a log home were cut and drug to a home site. Usually the site was near to where there was available timber.

Log homes were not to be found in Germany. There was such a shortage of timber that you cut no trees. Now tailors, cabinet makers, and cobblers were doing work they could not have imagined in Europe. The area of Perry County and Ste. Genevieve county had many Indians. The Osage and the Shawnee had been building log homes and barns for decades. The Osage built their structures with logs placed vertically. The Shawnee placed their logs horizontally.

The immigrants worked together. They came from the same area in Germany and that was an advantage, for families that could have a conversation with other folks from Germany. After all, to use a crosscut saw you needed two people. The immigrants to The Ridge needed each other.

There was a sawmill along Brazeau Creek. To purchase enough lumber to build a home took about fifty dollars. Who had that much money?

The people on The Ridge came looking for a better life. They came in a relatively short period of time and they came from the same area of Germany, Hanover. Of importance they were of the same religion, they were Lutheran. All of this helped them stay together. They did not need to learn a new language. They all spoke German. It would take to generations before this changed. The people were suddenly transplanted from a cultured and well-regulated life to a life filled with hardships. Plus, they had to make many adjustments to life. People are individuals, all different, some more inventive than others, some stronger than others, some had strong traits of leadership, while this quality lacked in others. They now found themselves in America and back on The Ridge. They needed each other if they were to survive.

The Lutheran faith plays an important role in the lives of these people. The Ridge people journeyed to Altenburg for worship. There they met other Lutherans, Germans at that, who had survived and now were seeing success on their farms. That success encouraged The Ridge folks.

They did not know it at the time but they would come through this a strong people. People would emerge on The Ridge who were remarkable in what they accomplished in a short period of time.

The Ridge, initially called *Friedland* is a unique place. Because of its location it developed into a community somewhat different then the Altenburg-Frohna area. One sees some things much the same but The Ridge produced a toughness not found elsewhere in Perry County. The Ridge folks are always German, always, Lutheran, always tough and hard working and *im mer Deutsche*.

SOURCES

1. This Chapter is from many documents at the Lutheran Heritage Center and Museum in Altenburg, Missouri.

2. One Furrow at A Time, Charles Rauh.

Chapter 2
Building the First Houses

(canstockphoto.com)

Let us get on with our history. Just how did these folks enter a new country and arrive in this hilly corner of Perry County and make a beginning? Today we know they succeeded. How? Can a cobbler become a farmer and pioneer? Keep reading and learn how this took place. Let us begin with housing.

The early settlers on The Ridge did not starve. There were berries to pick. One found plenty of mulberry trees. The early folks built crude rabbit traps and supplemented their diet. With a rifle they could shoot a deer. It wasn't much but it was a meal.

Photo courtesy of Lutheran Heritage Center and Museum,
Altenburg, MO

The other major need was shelter. You only had to do this once but it was quite an effort. Earlier we learned that the Indians were building log houses and barns. Think about it. Where do you get buffalo hide to make a tent on The Ridge? A deer skin was too small. So, the Indians cleared ground and took logs to build shelters. They also cleared ground by burning off timber. When the Ridge folks arrived, they found some already cleared fields. However, the Indians had moved to Kansas by the time the first Saxons arrived in 1839.

The Shawnee Indians lived in large numbers along Apple Creek south of Altenburg. They farmed and raised horses and cattle. They were known to even cut hay and put it in their barn lofts. No doubt the early settlers copied from the Indians. They did not know of logs being used for building in Germany. Now the tailors and cobblers had to learn log construction.

The people worked together. After all, remember it takes two men to operate a cross-cut saw. They lacked tools and had to make do with what they had. To get homes built they had to work together. To build a log home required the combined effort of men to transport logs. Early on there were very few horses or oxen to pull logs. Men had to literally pick them up and carry them. Now you know why the logs were small in the early log homes.

When the log got to the building site the bark was peeled off with great care. A chalk line was struck to delineate the exact thickness of the finished log, the thickness varied from six to eight inches. After there was a chalk line on the sides of the logs, they were notched with an ax to the chalk line every eighteen inches on both sides. The wood between these notches was split off. This took precision work to cut these notches deep enough but not too deep, else you weakened the log. After this, the broad axe was used. This separated the men from the boys. To make a clean, smooth cut, one that an adult not be ashamed of, took a hefty swipe with enough force to go through, and not only accurately, it has to be exactly accurate. For the best results, it took two men for this job, one to hold the log steady, while the other did the hewing.

After all the logs were hewn and finished, the house was "blocked up" or, as it was called, "raised". For this work all the neighbors, relatives, and friends were invited. Since the first round of logs needed precision and they were close to ground level, these were usually laid the day before with a small experienced crew.

For the "raising" proper the hewn logs were carefully measured and cut off at the exact mark by two men who could handle a crosscut saw and make a clean square cut. But the men who make the greatest importance and attracted the most attention were the four "corner hacks". These were men who knew how to handle an axe and how to keep their axe sharp. These corner hacks were stationed one at each corner of the building and it was their duty to cut the dovetails on the corners. If a man had earned the reputation that he could cut corners well, he had it made and was held in high regard.

A corner hack could construct a perfect hack. Each cut was so well done that the water drained out and nobody could remove a log on the building without dismantling the entire building above the log that you wished to remove. Usually the corner hacks also were the type of men that had a big chaw of tobacco between their teeth and cheek. They were as accurate spitting as they were using an axe.

Getting logs to the building site was tough work. If the logs you cut were up hill from the site, men with ropes could more easily move them. The Ridge was so hilly that this was often the case. The men drug logs or simply carried them. The logs were cut to the approximate length to be used in order to reduce the weight. Now you know why logs used in a log home were smaller logs and not the very large type. At the home site and as the home got taller ropes were used to pull the logs higher, at a certain point poles with a forked end were used to help push up the logs.

From oral history there were few serious accidents. Occasionally there was a mashed finger and bruised hands. The goal was to build a home and no one receiving even a black fingernail. If a home was built without serious injury it was custom for everyone to stand together and sing, "Nun danket alle Gott" - Martin Rinckart, 1636.

A home raising was hard work for the men involved. The owner provided the food with the women bringing a dish. They ate a noon and evening meal with a mid-morning *lunch* and an afternoon *lunch*. That tradition continued and was also done with the threshing rings. The Ridge folks always ate well.

If it were possible the logs used were taken from an area the farmer wanted to use for a field to grow crops. When the home was built the farmer went to work clearing the field. A grubbing hoe was a must tool, the small sprouts were grubbed out. The large trees were girded (a ring cut around the tree). The tree would eventually die and rot. When the tree was dead it was usually cut down and used for firewood. The farmer grew crops between the stumps. Later when there were horses and mules the stumps were grubbed and the roots sawed. The horses pulled the stump out of the ground and it was burned.

After a field was cleared it was planted with corn. When the corn was ripe the corn was brought in to the barn, stalks, shucks, and all. Nothing was wasted. The animals would eat the shucks in the winter. When molasses was available the shucks were sprinkled with molasses to get the animals to eat.

Wheat fields were also planted. The farmer plowed around the stumps. Crude harrows were used to smooth the field. The seed was broadcast (by hand) and harrowed again to cover the seed.

If you were lazy and abhorred hard work, the Ridge was no place for you.

The important thing is they got it done. These cobblers, linen weavers and hatters got it done. They did not have the word "quit" in their vocabulary. When we look back on the accomplishments of these immigrants we just shake our heads and say, "they did it!"

SOURCES

1. This chapter is drawn from previous writing by Theodore Popp.

2. The *Encyclopedia Britannica* was consulted.

Chapter 3
Firewood

Cutting firewood with a bucksaw.
From: tumblerose.com

The early years at the Ridge did not know of the future of natural gas, coal, or electricity. These modern conveniences would come later. Early on the only source of fuel was wood.

Throughout the year trees would be blow down by a storm or a tree would finally die. These were the trees that would be used for firewood to heat the house and heat the kitchen stove.

When cold weather came on the farm it was time to do nothing but wait for spring. Right? Wrong! It was time to cut firewood. Grandpa did such things as sharpen sickle blades, sharpen the mowing scythe, or mending harnesses. His boys were dispatched to cut firewood.

This was hard work on the Ridge. All farmers had to do this or freeze in the winter. So, did my Grandpa. Grandpa would decide which trees would be sawed and brought to the house. The two sons had long since learned how to use a crosscut saw and a one man crosscut saw. The work began.

The wood would be sawed into lengths that would fit into the heating stove. There also was wood to be cut to fit into the kitchen stove.

When the sawing began the sons just knew the length, they didn't have to measure. Believe it or not, even if the temperature was below freezing you could work up a sweat. It was hard work. If your partner on one corner of the crosscut was able, it was not as hard. There is an art to using a crosscut saw.

The wood was sawed and piled. Once piled, at the end of one day it was loaded and hauled to the house. As the winter progressed the pile dwindled. The pile had to last through the winter and the next summer. Occasionally Grandma came out to the wood pile and offered her comments.

The story is told that along the Ridge main road there was a farmer that noticed someone was stealing wood off his wood pile. Consider all the work involved to produce the pile of firewood one can appreciate his displeasure. The farmer decided to stop wood stealing. He took a quarter stick of dynamite and put it inside of firewood. In a few weeks the stick of wood was gone. A week or two later the farmer was in

Altenburg to have his plow shares and harnesses repaired at the blacksmith shop. One the side wall sat a heating stove with a hole in the side. Grandpa asked who's stove it was. He was told the name and that the man's son placed part of a stick of dynamite in the stove as a trick on his dad. Grandpa knew. He later confronted the man and the firewood stealing stopped.

Life on the Ridge was not easy. Even such a fundamental thing as keeping warm in the winter and cooking all year long requires a lot of hard work. There was sawing, stacking at the site, and later stacking at the house. Lest we forget there was splitting the large pieces. If the pieces were very large a wedge and sledge hammer was used to split it.

Today it is turning a knob on a kitchen stove and you cook with gas or electricity. Adjust the thermostat and we heat with gas or electricity. Not on The Ridge in the 1950's and before. We take it for granted keeping our homes warm and cooking with modern appliances but back then it was hard work. The folks on The Ridge knew nothing else.

Today we do all we can to get out of work. We spend our time figuring how to avoid work. Think about this, the early folks enjoyed "work". They got up and began a day's "work". "Work" was what they knew. "Work" was what they did. They worked until their hands bled. They did that so that today our hands don't have to bleed.

SOURCES

Personal experiences

Chapter 4
Raising Hogs and Other Stuff

**(meatsandsausages.com/public/images/smokehouses/
smokehouse-old-monroe-kitchen.jpg)**

The Ridge folks were hill farmers. A short drive from
Wittenberg to the former site of Weber's Store will convince you
of that fact. This was difficult farming. One can only imagine
the hard work that went into clearing ground so fields could be
planted. The ridge farmers were *general farmers*. This is to say
they did not specialize. Out west there are wheat farmers. Even
hay farmers dot the west raising only hay. In Iowa and Illinois
there exist farmers that only plant corn. Not so on the Ridge.
On the Ridge a farmer raised everything. There was wheat,

barley, oats, cows, hogs, chickens, and much more. Some farms had a small flock of geese and ducks. You could find farms with guinea and bantam chickens. The Ridge had it all.

The farms on the Ridge had what were called cash crops. These were crops that could be converted to cash when sold. All this provided there was something left to sell.

Wheat was a cash crop. There was a mill in Wittenberg and the mill would purchase all the wheat in the area. Bread was made from flour. Wheat was in high demand.

Hogs were a source of cash. There was a ready market for hogs. Because of the demand most every farm had a herd of hogs. To raise hogs, you needed corn. Ridge farmers planted a lot of corn for this purpose. Each farm had a boar to breed the females.

Hogs on The Ridge varied in type according to the wish of the farmer. Many hogs were black. These were Poland, China or Berkshire. Some farmers thought white hogs were more susceptible to skin disease. Some farmers raised red hogs. People claimed the red hogs had more fat which makes them harder to sell.

After pigs were weaned they were called shoats. The shoats now had to mature. They were not slopped or fed much at all. Many farmers let shoats roam in the woods. The shoats finally made it into the hog pen. Now they were slopped and received corn. Shoats in the hog pen could quickly find a weak place in the pen and crawl out. The chase would begin.

Seldom was a hog butchered that was less than a year old. People said the meat did not taste right. Usually they were butchered when about 12 months old. A farmer knows to stay away from sows. Sows are generally in a foul mood. If you approached a sow, the sow would show you mean looking dentures. No one, yet no one, got into the sow pen.

In the early years sows were known to have their litter of pigs in the woods. They simply found a pile of leaves and gave birth. Again, you should stay away from the sow. Woods pigs had an advantage. They would have no lice. Pigs raised on straw would have lice. Some farmers gathered sacks of leaves and put the leaves in the hog house for the sow to deliver her pigs.

Today hogs are fed all sorts of supplements. Not in the early years. If there was extra milk after the milk separating, the hogs would be fed the milk. They also were fed all the table scraps. They got ear corn. When the farmers could afford a corn grinder the diet changed. Corn was ground and, in a barrel, it was mixed with water. This slop went into the hog trough.

All of this work was for one purpose. To get the hogs ready for butchering in the winter. Any excess hogs would be sold to a ready market.

On a farm on The Ridge it doesn't seem you ever had your work completed.

SOURCES

1. Drawn from the work of Theo. Pop

2. Personal Experience

Chapter 5
Schwartenmägen
Blütwurst - Leberwurst - Bratwurst und Gritzawurst

(meatsandsausages.com/public/images/smokehouses/
smokehouse-old-monroe-kitchen.jpg)

If you slopped your hogs and fed them corn you had hogs to be butchered in the winter. This was an exciting time. As a nine-year-old boy I experienced butchering day.

Usually you butchered hogs with another family. Four to six hogs were common. This made for plenty of work for everyone. The day began before daylight. The kettles were in place. Plenty of wood was nearby to heat these. They were filled with water and the fires were lit. Everything needed was set up the day before. The scalding vat was in place. The gambling sticks were accounted for.

Very early the neighbors arrived, they drove their hogs to the farm and into a hog pen. By now the kettles were boiling. The men stood around the fire and discussed what they always talk about, the weather. No one knew how to change it. By now it was daylight and time to go to work. The kettles all got another bucket of water or two. The fires received more wood. The men then went to the hog pen to kill the hogs. The hogs, the poor things, had no notion that their short life was all for the purpose of providing food for a kitchen table.

There was always someone who was known as an excellent shot with a twenty-two rifle. To kill a hog the bullet needed to be exactly between the hogs' eyes. In my family my uncle was always chosen to kill the hogs.

The rifle cracked and a hog fell dead. The hog was rolled over and a man rammed a knife into the throat of the hog. Blood gushed out and it was saved to later be used to provide color for blood sausage (blutwurst). The same procedure followed until all the hogs were killed. I was amazed as to what I was watching.

One man was assigned to take care of the blood. It was put into a crock and taken to the smokehouse to be used later. When this man had his assignment completed he then helped with the scalding.

Meanwhile the dead hogs were drug to the scalding vat or barrel. The vat was a wooden trough about twenty-four inches wide and twenty inches deep. It was five feet long. Chains or usually ropes were laid across the trough. The hog was laid on top. Men took the ropes and began to swish the hog up and down. This was all done to remove the hair. If a barrel was used this was propped up on a slant and full of scalding water. The hog was put in the barrel head first and swished. Then the hog was reversed to remove hair. Scrapers were used to removed any remaining hair.

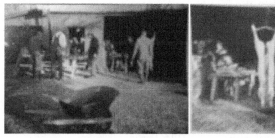

Photos courtesy of Flora Stueve Kassel

While the men moved the first hog along, other men secured and scalded the next hog. The men had to work quickly. The first hog had its hind legs slashed to expose the tendons. Through the openings the gambling sticks were inserted. The hog was hung on a beam, meanwhile the scrapers continued their work.

It is now that the head was removed. This was thoroughly cleaned. The eyes were removed. The head was cut up, the brains were removed and saved, and the meat placed in kettles to be boiled.

Next came the remaining of the entrails. One of the men separated these, washed and boiled them in salt water. These would later be used for sausage casings.

Meat was continuously going into the kettles to be boiled. It would later go through a grinder and used in sausage.

By now it was time for lunch. You will not believe the meal. It was scrambled eggs mixed with hog brains. I was reluctant but after trying it, I could eat it.

It was time after lunch to cut up the hogs. The hams, shoulders, bacon sides, spareribs, and back bone (loin) were cut out. Now all that was left was sausage meat and boiling lard. The sausage meat was cut into small pieces and ground. The person assigned to the handle on the grinder could work up a sweat. This became much easier work when in 1945 the area received electricity. Then an electric grinder could be used.

Sausage making began in earnest. Usually there was one of the men who was considered the best in seasoning sausage. After he started his work grandma come out and told him that last year he used to much pepper. He simply nodded and continued his work.

Salt and pepper were the basic seasonings in all sausages. Mustard, whole mustard seed, some liking yellow and some black and some added caraway seed to get the correct amount of these seasonings. How all of this tasted depended on the skill of the sausage maker. Head cheese (*schwartenmägen*) was made first because it went into the hog's stomach. This required a longer boiling period.

Next came the blood sausage (*blütwurst*). Into this sausage went the boiled lungs, the darker meat, the very fat part, strips of the lower or under sides. This was coarsely ground, seasoned with salt, pepper, and marjoram. Some added mustard seed and enough blood to give it a desired color. This was put into the large stomach casing, put into a kettle and boiled. After a time, you pricked the casing. You needed clean liquid and the sausage was completed.

Liver sausage (*leberwurst*) was the last of the cooked sausages. The liver was previously cooked. Now it is ground very fine. The meat left from the head and other fat meats were added. Most people used only salt and pepper to season the mixture. The mixture was stuffed into casings and cooked.

The sausage makers now saw to making fry sausage (*bratwurst*). Sausage meat was seasoned with salt and pepper. Some used coriander to season while some added sage. In fact, each household had their own recipe.

Much of this sausage was stuffed into small casings, but some of it was made by hand into meatballs and fried down and stuffed into crocks. In later years it was placed into quart jars and stored in a cool place such as the cellar.

The kettles were now emptied to be used for rendering the lard. This process had to be closely watched. If it was not rendered enough the lard soured and spoiled. If it was rendered a little too long it turned to a shade of brown and it would have a scorched flavor. The women did not hesitate to step in and give orders. Women supervised the rendering much to the chagrin of their husbands.

A large supper ended the day. All the meat and especially the sausages were sampled. The neighbor loaded his half of everything on his wagon and went home.

The meat, hams, shoulders and sides, were put in the smoke house. The sausages were also put in the smoke house and hung up on broom handles. The next day after the meat had cooled it could now be cured. Some cured with brine and others used the dry cure method. Both were good methods and the meat tasted equally good. Every family had their own method for seasoning and curing. After the meat was cured, it was smoked. Some smoked slowly while others smoked with a hotter system. Both methods were good. Some used only hickory wood for smoking. If the fire got to hot moist wood was used to slow things down.

When the butchering took place, the weather was cold. Often it was spitting snow. With the cold wind blowing the men saw the need for a warmer-upper. This liquid was near 100% proof and came in a brown bottle. As soon as the hogs were killed and were being scalded the bottle was passed around. All the men took a "pull" out of the bottle. Remember, it is now just after daylight. The "pulls" had to be in moderation, if one was to make it all day. Of course, the women were not to know about the bottle. Who was kidding whom? In order to endure the cold a sip was necessary about every top of the hour.

Butchering on The Ridge was necessary for food for the family, it was a social event, it was hard work, it was fun work, and it was an experience a nine-year-old boy would never forget. And now, seventy years later I get to write about the day I "helped" butcher.

There is a story that needs to be told. It is a true story in every respect. I was nine years old at the time but the memory is as if it was yesterday. My parents journeyed to Martin Stueve's farm. Dad and mom would help with the butchering. The other family involved was the neighbor, Albert Leimbach.

The butchering was underway. The hogs had been shot and scalded. I was cold. I stood next to a kettle in order to get warm. I stood too close and too long. My pant leg caught fire. When I saw it, my Grandpa Martin saw it, simultaneously. I started to ruin for the house. Grandpa yelled for me to stand still. I kept running, Grandpa caught and tackled me. He then took his bare hands and put the burning material out. With that done he took his hands and tore the corduroy smoldering material off my leg. Before he could grab my hands, I grabbed the burned area to rub it. This rubbing probably increased the scar which today I have on my leg.

Grandpa picked me up in his arms and took me to the house. The women were aghast. Grandma went immediately to work while my mother tired console me. Grandma mixed lard, butter and maybe other things. The mixture was put on the burned leg and wrapped with one of my brother's diapers. I was put into bed. Dad was not about to leave the butchering and return to Jackson. I laid in bed and eventually settled down. One thing about a nine-year-old being injured. I got all the cookies and milk I could hold.

The next day dad took me to Jackson to see a doctor. It was Dr. Rusby Seabaugh. He examined the leg and told dad that what grandma put on the burn was just fine. A prescription was written and dad was told to clean the area of the burn and grandma's poultice and apply the new ointment.

I was nine years old. The scar on the calf of my right leg is the shape of a nine. Hmmm!

It happened on The Ridge. Life was certainly different in those early years. Ridge folks worked hard, played hard, and helped each other. This tiny community tucked away in east Perry County need to never be forgotten.

SOURCES

1. Drawn from work by Theo. Popp

2. Encyclopedia Britannica

Chapter 6
Making Apple butter

Photo courtesy of Eileen Wichern

Life on the Ridge was certainly a far different life then we know today. If there is a word to describe the life of Ridge people it is self-sufficiency. Self-sufficiency was a matter of principle and to a large extent a matter of pride. There was no money. Yet people wanted to dress in clean, nice clothes. They also wanted to eat well. No one wanted to go into debt because the lack of money made it difficult to repay a loan. People on the Ridge

27

boasted, "I owe no man." Because of this pride people learned to do without money. They learned to do without many things. The Ridge people worked hard and took pride in saying that they went six months without spending money.

My mother told me a story about not spending money. During the Depression there was certainly no money. She said the family went one year without spending a cent. Necessary spices, salt, and needles and thread, were purchased with egg money. For Christmas each member of the family personally made a gift for a member of the family. Mom said, "the best Christmas we ever had."

There were certain customs on the Ridge. The customs had a sound purpose and were designed to save money. Butchering was one of the customs. Another was apple butter making.

The old saying that an apple a day keeps the doctor away is probably as old as the apple. To bite into a ripe juicy apple is as good as it gets. Bite into and eat a green apple can be a horrendous experience. The stomach feels like it is being twisted and the trips to the outhouse are numerous.

In the early years on the Ridge there were no quart jars. Canning fruit was not practiced. Some folks dried fruit, put it in crocks, and ate the fruit in the winter.

Making apple butter became popular. Jellies and preserves were about fifty percent sugar. Purchasing sugar was expensive. When apple butter was cooked one used only two pounds of sugar to the gallon.

All of the Ridge farms had their own small orchard. Usually there was a cherry tree, a couple varieties of peach trees, sometimes a plum tree, and there was a variety of apple trees. The peach tree of choice was the Elberta.

There was a variety of apple trees. There were early apples and winter apples. A farmer had a yellow apple tree and a red apple tree. Some apples ripened during the summer. These were not desired apples. The apples everyone wanted were winter apples which ripened late and had the ability to last through the winter. For eating and cider making the Winesap was the choice. For apple butter the Ben Davis was supreme.

There is a debate as to why summer apples were not used for apple butter. Some say it was because there was too much farm activity during the summer and there was no time for apple butter making. Or was it because summer apples were conducive to making good apple butter. Then there are some that say it is too hot around the kettle in the summer to fool with apple butter. Generally, apple butter cooking happened late in the fall and winter apples were used.

When threshing and hay hauling were complete it was time to cook apple butter. The children in the family took baskets and buckets and picked up apples on the ground. If dad allowed, the boys climbed up into the trees to pick more apples. With ten-year-old boys who needs a ladder?

The first day of apple butter cooking was spent peeling apples. The apples were peeled and cut into quarters. The peeling was done in one of two ways. One could use a paring knife. The champion peeler was one who could peel the entire apple and have the skin in one long piece. The other method was an apple peeler. This was hand cranked. Electricity had not yet reached the Ridge. The apple peeler was fastened to a table, the apple was fixed to a small-tined fork on the peeler, then by turning the handle, the apple was rotated against the knife. The peeler took only a thin piece of peeling off of the apple. Originally these peelers were provided with an arm that would automatically eject the apple from the fork after it was peeled but after a few years these ejectors broke. After that, the person who operated the peeler had to pull the peeled apple from the fork by hand.

After the apples were peeled and cut into pieces, they were put into containers, wash tubs, milk buckets, or clean bushel baskets. They were covered with clean dish towels and saved until the next day for cooking. Woe to the child caught eating the apples.

In the German way of managing the farm, the husband made all the decisions. Except the apple butter cooking. His wife assumed command and her husband was ordered to stay out of the way. His wife did not want him even close to the kettles. He wasn't even allowed to stoke the fire under the kettle for fear he would get the fire too hot and scorch the apple butter. Dad's would find other things to do and leave the women to themselves.

The children of the family were to stay with mom and do her bidding. They carried in the firewood. Old fence posts were ideal. Mom could push them under the kettle as they burned down. That was how she controlled the heat. It was not too long that the children got either tired or bored. They would slip off and play leaving mom with all the work. If truth were known she liked it this way.

The day of the cooking everyone was up early. Mother went out on the front porch to check the weather. There was no television station to give you the forecast and there were no newspapers delivered. The evening prior she prayed hard for good weather. After fixing breakfast mother did a final cleaning of the kettle. The kettle was made of copper. Every family prized their kettle. Again, woe to a child who would put a dent in the kettle. A boy just might feel dad's razor strap. In the very early years a kettle cost eleven dollars. Quite a sum of money. The copper would tarnish. To clean the kettle required a lot of elbow grease. (Today at a farm auction you might pay up to $700 - 900.00 for one of these copper kettles.)

When all was ready the kettle was filled with water. The kettle sat on a tripod with the fire under the kettle. When the water was hot the apples were put inside. The contents had to be constantly stirred. The difficult part was to cook the apples as fast as possible without scorching the mixture. If apple butter was scorched mom always kept a couple of crocks good apple butter in case there was company. The family pride had to be maintained.

Not all the peeled apples were in the kettle. The cooking continued and more apples were added. Sometimes the mixture in the kettle would bubble on to the rim of the kettle. With a long-handled pot apple butter was ladled out and put in a container ready for this purpose.

Finally, the cooking settled down into a long boring day. Wherever the person stirring stood, it seemed the smoke from the fire went that direction. It seemed to always blow toward the shade tree.

The paddle used to stir the pot resembled an oversized hoe. The hoe part was about two feet long with large holes drilled into it. It had a long handle. It was long so the person doing the stirring did not have to stand close to the intense heat. As the mixture boiled, bubbles would form and pop. If it hit the stirrer on the arm a burn resulted.

It was after lunch. Time to add the sugar. About two pounds per estimated gallon. While it was being added the stirrer stirred quickly. Some added cinnamon powder or sticks. A few added anise.

When mother said that all was ready it got very busy. Before quart jars, crocks were used. These were all set in place. Now father and sons could help. A strong pole was put through and under the kettle bail or handle. The kettle was carefully taken off of the tripod and set on the ground exactly where mother wanted it.

The apple butter was now removed and put into crocks. A lid was placed on the crock and the crock sealed with paraffin wax. The crocks went to the cellar for cooling.

When one takes a piece of homemade bread and covers it with a half-inch of apple butter it makes all the work worth it.

That's how they did it on The Ridge in 1900.

SOURCES

1. Work by Theo. Popp

2. Various internet sources

Chapter 7
Soap Making

Apple Butter making took place in the fall of the year. So, did soap making. Mother was in charge of apple butter cooking and she was also in charge of soap making. Men just do not have the patience to do it correctly.

In the early years the word *detergent* was not yet in the dictionary. The Germans did not say soap, the said *seife*.

In 1900 everything was cleaned with lye soap. The floors were scrubbed with old rags and lye soap. The laundry was washed in the lye soap and the family took a bath with lye soap. Many households had a hand operated washing machine. If you did not have one you use a washboard and washtub. Most likely the washtub was made of wood.

There was an unwritten law on the Ridge. Monday is wash day. That means Tuesday is ironing day. Why? Who knows! The law was written by women and men are expected to obey it. If washing was not done on Monday the whole week was messed up. By the way, Saturday was bath day. I can understand this one. You wanted to smell good at church.

Beginning at butchering time, the inedible fats were saved and kept in crocks and stored in the cellar. This fatty meat was for the base of soap making.

Soap was always made in the fall. The weather had to be cool enough so the soap would harden the first night. Here now is another law written by mothers. Soap making needs to take place on a clear day. No one knows why. Everyone obeys the laws of mothers. I think the mothers would have thought Judgment Day had arrived if a rainstorm happened during soap making.

Before you can cook soap, you need lye. This was purchased at Fisher's Store in Altenburg. It cost twenty cents a can. In 1900 this was not a small amount. It is said that in the 1700's lye was made by pouring water on wood ashes.

To cook soap, you need a black cast iron kettle. Maybe two! The reason for two was that it took two batches to last a family for one year. The kettles sat on a tripod with a fire underneath.

After the water was heated in the kettles grease was added, while all this was taking place father and sons carried wood to the site.

The mothers were constantly stirring the water and grease mixture. At the right time (only mother knew when the time was right) a can of lye went into each kettle. This was also stirred, to make sure all the lye was used. The empty can was sunk into the kettle mixture. It would be retrieved later.

By now the fatty meat has been added. Now the process has to be carefully watched. The mixture needed a low boiling point. If it was boiled to little you got a poor-quality soap. If it was boiled too hard all sorts of thing could happen. The mixture would go wild and boil over. The stirrer knew when the job was done. When the paddle was lifted the mixture should not fall in drops but in thread-like strings. Usually the soap making was finished by noon.

Mother could now take a break. But first she had to go to the house and cook a noon meal. After the meal and the dishes washed and put away mother would go out and admire her work. She laid boards over the kettles in case it might rain. It is sad that once a kitten was walking on one of the boards. The cat slipped and fell into the kettle. A horrible death resulted.

Mother isn't done yet. The next morning, she went out with a corn knife or a large butcher knife and cut the hardened soap into blocks. Those were put on short boards and taken to the smoke house. Here the soap dried and cured.

When it was Saturday and you took your bath, you took the bath using mother's lye soap. I remember one verse of the Andy Griffith song "Grandma's Lye Soap".

> "Little Herman and brother Thurman had an aversion to washing their ears. Momma scrubbed them with lye soap and they haven't heard a word in years."

SOURCES

1. Work by Theo. Popp

2. Internet sources.

Chapter 8
Egg Money and Making Molasses

Molasses Factory, Altenburg, MO
Courtesy of Lutheran Heritage Museum, Altenburg, MO

If one is destined to live on very little income what does the person or family do to have certain house or farm supplies. During the years prior to World War I there was little money. If there were needs that required money, the items were simply not purchased.

This was life on the Ridge. A way to purchase basic needs, salt, pepper, other food staples and sewing needs a farmer would "trade in" eggs. You saved or cased eggs and took them to Fisher's store in Altenburg. The store counted the eggs and multiplied the number of eggs by the price per dozen. The customer now had money credit at the store to purchase basic needs. Some stores would give the seller currency for the eggs. The currency was in the form of wooden coins or paper certificates printed by the store. This system worked for many years.

People have a natural attraction to sweets. For the early Ridge settlers, sugar was unaffordable. Rarely did mom come home from Fishers Store with a store with a sack of sugar. Around Christmas time there would be sugar purchased so a cake or cookies could be baked.

Rather than use sugar there was a cheaper alternative. The product was molasses. Molasses was also called "the long sweetening". Farmers on the Ridge had a sugar cane patch. The patch was not large. Two acres of sugarcane would have been a lot. The patch would be in the back end of a field. New ground just cleared of trees was also a popular place to plant sugar cane.

Dad would plow a small area for the patch. Seed was planted by hand. Once the cane was growing the ground had to be plowed to keep the grass growing to a minimum. Sometimes the children were assigned hoeing duty. No better way to keep your childr3n busy than to have them work in the sugar cane patch.

Sugar cane work was not yet completed. When it rained hard some of the cane would be washed out. The children now had more work to do. The washed-out plants were gathered and transplanted in the open row spaces. Also, there were areas where the cane had been planted too thick. The row had to be thinned and the stacks replanted in thinly planted rows. When a young boy got up in the morning he hoped dad would not assign him duty in the cane patch.

When the cane was ripe the leaves had to be stripped from the stalk. The leaves were laid on the ground between the rows. The edges of the leaves were sharp. By the time the patch as finished the boys had all sorts of cuts on their arms and hands. No boy ever died from a sugar cane cut but he would show his cuts as a badge of honor.

When the stalks were stripped, the stalks had to be cut with a corn knife. The stalk had to be cut low near the ground. The bottom of the stalk was thick and held the most juice. Now the stalks would be hauled to the cane press.

The leaves which had been laid on the ground were gathered and taken to the barn to be fed to livestock during the winter. Nothing was wasted. The heads on the stalks were saved for seed for the next year.

The leaves which had been laid on the ground were gathered and taken to the barn to be fed to livestock during the winter. Nothing was wasted. The heads on the stalks were saved for seed for the next year.

Every community had a cane press. These were of a practical and simple design. There were three iron rollers. One was larger than the other two. They were placed vertical. There was a long pole on top of the press. A horse or mule was hitched to the pole to turn the rollers. While the horse turned the rollers, a farmer fed his cane stacks between the rollers.

Near the press was a shed for the molasses cooking pan. It was of a shallow design, about six feet wide and twelve feet long.

There were dividers every five or six inches across, to within about six inches from the other side. These openings alternated causing the juice to flow slowly across the heated pan. This pan was mounted on brick walls and the bricks formed the fireplace. This is where the molasses cooker worked.

The molasses cooker had an important jo to do. The cooker had to keep the cane juice at a high boiling point but the cooker had to take care so the juice would not be scorched. Scorching the juice ruined the flavor of the molasses.

If a farmer on the Ridge did not have a cane press, he had an alternative. He could load his cane and go to Frohna. Adolf Schirmer owned a press and would rent you time with his press. He also was a cobbler and made and repaired horse harnesses.

It was a great day when mom brought out the molasses for the family to sample. There was fresh baked bread to put the molasses on. Wow! This is the best ever!

SOURCES

1. Work by Theo. Popp

2. Internet Sources

3. Eileen Rauh

Chapter 9
CANNING VEGETABLES AND PRESERVING MEAT

The folks on the Ridge could not go to the store twice a week to purchase groceries. In the winter the body needs vegetables just like it does in the summer. How did they meet this need?

The farmer and the city or town people learned the art of canning. They early on knew how to preserve food. Who invented canning and when did canning begin? Would you believe it? Napoleon invented canning. Or at least he was involved. The canning process was first used in France.

Napoleon fought many wars. He needed a better way to feed his troops in the field. He offered a prize of 12,000 Francs to anyone who could devise such a means. Enter a man named Appert Earcier. It was believed that air caused food to spoil. Appert found that it was heat (caused by microbes) that was the culprit. He did not know anything about microbes.

Appert's process involved placing food in glass bottles. The bottles were corked just like wine and they were sealed with wax. Then the jars were wrapped in canvas and boiled. The French government announced that Appert won the prize in 1810.

In 1812, and Englishman, Brian Domicin substituted tin cans for jars. He called it unbreakable tin. The tin can industry was begun in 1812.

Just how safe is canned food? A steamboat sank in the Mississippi river some 100 years ago. When it was raised, a jar of canned food was found. The jar was opened and the food found edible.

In 1858, John Mason invented a canning jar. He invented a machine that could cut threads into lids which made lids reusable. His lid would mold into the top. He used a zinc lid with a rubber ring. The ring formed the seal. By 1858, the Ridge was being settled. Home canning was spreading across the United States.

Meanwhile in Buffalo, N.Y. William Ball, together with his brothers, were in the business of manufacturing wood-jacketed tin cans for the storage of oil, lard, and paints. In 1883 the Balls changed from tin to glass and then in 1886 to glass fruit jars. It was not long before they were the leaders of the jar industry.

Next came Alexander Kerr who came out with the first wide mouth jars. They caught on because they were easier to fill.

Canning jars swept across the nation everyone was involved in home canning. Whenever a vegetable ripened in the garden it was time to can. Not only vegetables but also meats. From liver sausage, to beef cubes were canned. Where do you think kettle cooked beef came from? I wonder how many glass canning jars were stored on each farm. There were also tiny glass jars for jelly and jam You could purchase jars from four ounces to one half gallon size jars.

A trip down into the cellar was a sight to behold. Hundreds of jars all filled. It all tasted *ohh* so good!

That's how the Ridge people survived. They didn't have the money to go to Fisher's store and buy food. They canned until the jars ran out.

There is more. How did the early folks on the Ridge preserve meat? They did it by salting and brining. This process was learned long ago in Saxony.

This old method of preserving meat is not difficult and takes little time. Following is the quick and simple method:

- Cut your meat into 4-inch to 6-inch slabs. Generally, for every 12 pounds, use 1/2 pound of pickling salt and ¼ cup of brown sugar. Coat all the pieces with the salt mixture.

- Sterilize a 2-gallon or two 1-gallon crocks. To sterilize, wash and rinse it well with boiling water.

- Pack the meat tightly in the crocks and cover it tightly with cheesecloth.

- Keep the meat at 36-degrees Fahrenheit. No more than 38-degrees, no lower than freezing for at least a month. Wrap the meat in moisture-proof paper. It will keep all winter.

Now let's brine pork:

- Pack the pieces of pork in a sterilized crock or jar and cover with a brine of 3 quarts water, 1-pound pickling salt and ½ cup of brown sugar. Be sure the salt and sugar are dissolved.

- The brine must cover every inch of the meat, so if it doesn't, weigh it down with a heavy object like a quart jar full of water. Cover the container and store for a week at 36-degrees Fahrenheit.

- Remove the meat, stir the brine, and repack each week for 4 weeks. If the brine is thick or stringy, wash each piece of pork thoroughly, re-sterilize the container, and mix fresh brine.

Nice job! Now you have brined pork.

That's how they did it on the Ridge. If you today do not like cooking, gardening, or working in the kitchen, then life on the Ridge wasn't for you. The women worked long hours just like the men. You learned your trade from your mother and grandmother. They didn't complain about life, they enjoyed life. When electricity came along and a new kerosene cook stove, they were excited.

The first two needs were food and shelter. The men provided the shelter, the women provided the food. The men threshed, harvested hay, plowed, picked corn, and on and on. The women cooked, washed, ironed, hoed the garden and on and on. Life on the Ridge offered hard work, close families, friendly and helpful neighbors, fun at times, and joy in knowing you were a part of a Christian community.

SOURCES

1. Work by Theo. Popp

2. Internet Sources

3. Eileen Rauh

Chapter 10
CUTTING WHEAT AND THE BINDER

Courtesy of Lutheran Heritage Center & Museum

In the early years, the Ridge folks had no horses. Horses cost thirty dollars each and no one could afford a horse or mule. The first draft animal was an ox. It would not be long when every farmer had two horses. Some had four, especially if he had sons to help with the work. Remember, the more horses there were, the more it took to feed them.

Planting wheat was done in early fall. The goal on the Ridge was to have the wheat sewn by the end of September. This gave the wheat time to appear before winter. In the early years, a farmer could expect thirty bushels to the acre. This compares today to one hundred bushels to the acre.

The wheat harvest was begun in the month of June. It was done in the same way as they did it in Germany. They used a mowing scythe. The wheat was cut and with a special hand rake, it was raked into swaths. Now the person who made bundles began his work. That person tied the bundles. Now the shocking began. Every shock had twelve bundles. The bundles were stood upright. Then two bundles were used to cap the shock. Farmers took pride in well built shocks.

Now you know why a farmer wanted sons and not daughters!

It was not long and the cradle was invented. They always looked for a better way. This was not very scientific. They took a mowing scythe and attached a well-balanced frame. The frame had four wooden fingers about the length of the scythe blade. The fingers were like tines on a fork. The operator swung his scythe and the wheat (barley and oats) fell against the tines. After each swipe, the operator would grab the cut wheat and lay it in a windrow. The rake was now not needed. A farmer took great pride in his work and his well-balanced cradle.

Before threshing machines, the wheat was hauled to the barn and stacked. The wheat was stacked in such a manner so the heads of the grain were to the inside of the stack. This prevented the rain from soaking the grain. Lest it not be mentioned, the two bundles that capped the shock also kept the rain from soaking the bundles.

We are yet in the time before threshing machines. The early threshing was done with a flail. This was a simple implement. It was a piece of wood about four feet long. A leather loop was attached to one end. The other part was a piece of wood about thirty inches long. A leader strap was attached to one end in such a manner that the two loops inter-looped each other. The Israelites in the Old Testament most likely used this same tool.

Next came other new inventions. They always looked for a better and easier way. The first was a contrivance which had a contraption of gears applied power to a pulley, the power coming from horses being hitched to a long pole, going around and around.

Then a threshing machine appeared. It was similar to the threshing machines we know of that were used in the 1940's. But the first of these were much smaller. They were made of wood. There was no feeder or straw blower. The first of these were lifted on a wagon and transported from one farm to another. This threshing took a lot of man power but was less work then flailing. Neighbors had to help neighbors. It now becomes apparent why the Ridge folks were a close-knit people. You needed neighbors to help build your log home and needed them to help with threshing.

Cyrus McCormick invented the reaper in 1831. The reaper cut the grain and left it lay on the ground, but it still had to be hand tied. It took three or four hand-tiers for each reaper. A reaper made a round in the field. The tiers followed. The reaper would make four rounds to a tier's one round. Not all farmers could own their own reaper. Reapers were shared. The wheat still had to be shocked.

I remember asking my grandfather what the greatest invention was he saw in his life time. I thought he would say electricity or the tractor. He told me it was the binder. The first binder came in 1876. The first binder tied the bundles with wire. The wires would get into the straw. Animals would eat them and die. The wire binders did not last long. In 1888 string tying binders made their appearance on the Ridge. A knotter was invented. This invention was a great factor on insuring food supply not only for the country, but also the world.

Soon many farmers owned a binder. Sometimes, as did my grandfather, one was shared between two farms. Before McCormick and Deering, there was McCormick and there was Deering. Later they merged. The first binders that tied with string cost a farmer $116.00.

Before there could be threshing machines that we remember from the 1900's, there had to be steam engines. The first were placed on a heavy wagon and moved from place to place with a team of horses. This steam engine necessitated there be a water wagon. Water also would have to be hauled. These engines were a vast improvement over horse power.

The steam engine was hailed as a great invention. If the people did not appreciate this invention, I bet the horses did. When the self-propelled steam engine came along, it created a problem. When this huge black machine came down a road and met a team of mules, one just stopped and watched the fun. The mules just couldn't handle this giant in front of them. Sometimes the mules had to be turned and taken to an open field and let the iron giant pass.

As a boy of twelve years old, I spent two weeks on the Ridge with my grandpa and my two uncles working in the threshing ring. I pitched bundles in the field. This would have been in 1949-1950. Wow! What an experience. Also, there was those lunches brought to the field.

My partner pitching bundles was Hem Brauner. He taught me the correct way to pitch bundles so the driver on the wagon did not have to retstack the load. At the end of two weeks to my surprise, I was paid. I made twelve dollars a week. Not Bad!

SOURCES

1. Enclyclopedia Britanica

2. Internet

3. Theo. Popp

4. Personal Experiences

Chapter 11
Threshing

Around the turn of the century, threshing took a turn. The steam engine was mobile. The threshing machine had feeders and blowers. An individual could not afford a steam engine and a threshing machine. Either the community purchased these machines or an individual purchased a steam engine, threshing machine, and a water wagon. If it was an individual, he would charge each farmer so much a bushel to thresh his grain. At the Ridge, the investor in the threshing equipment was Ed Leimbach initially. Later it was the Brauner brothers. Ed Leimbach was elected as a county judge. Today they are called commissioners. On his right hand he was missing four fingers. He was left with his index finger. I remember as a boy seeing him pick up a five-gallon-bucket of water with that finger and walk off with it. I was amazed. You try it sometime.

Organized threshing rings came on the scene. The Ridge had the Ed Leimbach ring. When it was threshing time a lot of organization and preparation took place. The order of threshing was the same each year. The order was determined to go from one farm to the other and have the least travel time for the steam engine. When the threshing started, two men were assigned to measure the grain. The grain came out into a shallow box. The grain was measured with two half bushel buckets. Two men saw to filling the buckets and two or three men were assigned to be grain carriers. Each carrier made a mark with a pencil each time he carried two buckets or one bushel. The farmer and threshing machine owner now knew how many bushels of grain were threshed. The grain was now in a sack ready to be hauled to the granary. With wheat and barley, they put a full bushel into each sack. Oats sacks got one and a half.

Out in the field were bundle pitchers. The driver of the wagon pulled up to the shocks. He tied the reins to the ladder. Most horses only had to get the sound from the driver and they moved to more shocks. They simply knew where to go. On a steep hill the driver got involved. The bundle pitcher, two to a wagon, always put the bundles on the wagon butt last. When loaded, the driver took his load to the threshing machine. He waited his turn and then pulled up alongside the bundle feeder. The driver unloaded his bundles. He was not to put the bundles into the feeder too quickly lest he choke the machine. All sorts of cursing began when the machine was chocked! On top of the threshing machine sat a man who moved the blower. The straw came out of the blower and the straw stack was built. Building the stack was an art. The major problem for the man on the blower was when the wind changed direction and the dust blew into his face.

I recall one day in the field, I was pitching bundles with Hem Brauner. My uncle was pitching on a different wagon. He wanted to show off. We were loading oats bundles. He yelled at me to watch. He stuck in his pitch fork and was going to pick up the whole shock. I was watching. When he lifted up the shock a black snake fell out and landed on his neck! He got busy very quickly!

At noon, everyone went to the house to eat. The ladies helped each other. Each knew when and where they were to help. When you sat at the table, you could not believe the food. Always three or four different meats. All the vegetables the garden grew, and enough potatoes to feed an army. The owner of the farm offered a prayer, all of the dialogue at the table was in German, including the prayer. If you want to learn the German language you have to work in a threshing ring on the Ridge. If you wanted something on the table, you needed to know how to ask for it in German. My grandpa, Martin Stueve, was a kind and gentle man. Without a doubt he was a Christian gentleman! There was an African American man that lived on the Ridge. He wanted work and he asked Grandpa if he could work for him during threshing. Grandpa said yes. This man was assigned to help hall grain to the granary. It came time for the noon meal. Everyone wondered where this man would eat. Certainly not at the main table. Grandpa knew what was on everyone's mind. Before the men went into the house Grandpa got everyone's attention. He told the men that any man who would work for him could sit at his table. The black went into the house and grandpa seated him. No one said a word then or after. To tell this story today makes me very proud of Martin Stueve. The year was 1949 and *it happened on the Ridge!*

SOURCES

1. Theo. Popp

2. Internet

3. Personal Experience

Chapter 12
Hay Hauling

Courtesy of the Martin Stueve Family

You don't know what hot is until you have stacked hay under the tin roof of the barn hay loft. When the temperature reaches 100 degrees and the hay has been cut and raked it is time to haul hay. In the 1940's there were no machines to bale the hay. The hay was hauled loose.

When it was time for hay hauling, there were no television stations to give you a weather forecast. You could not even get a weather report on the radio. Grandpa was the weather forecaster. At best, his forecasts were a guess.

One of the boys was told to cut hay. The mower was the riding kind. Grandpa had sharpened the sickle blades. One of the sons took the mower to the clover field and cut the lush green hay.

Following the cutting, came the raking. Before tractors and the side delivery rake, the farmers used the "dump-rake". With the team of horses, the dump-rake gathered the hay. The rider on the rake pulled a lever and dumped the hay in what was called a windrow. This would be left to dry before being loaded and brought to the barn. Grandpa never wanted to see rain on the newly cut hay. Wet hay will mold. If this hay is in the barn loft it will heat up as it molds. This can cause spontaneous combustion, which in the end burns the barn to the ground.

It is probably the hottest day of the year. This heat affects the men who will have to work the hay and it affects the horses or mules. To haul the hay the wagon used was called the *hay frame*. It had no sides. On the front and back was what was called *the ladders*. These lay flat on the hay frame wagon bed. They would be raised for hay hauling.

Young Charlie, about ten years old, is visiting his grandfather's farm for the week. He will get to help haul hay!

Grandpa, his two sons Norbert and Harry and Charlie were on the way to the hayfield. By the time you got there, you had already worked up a sweat. It was hotter than blue blazes!

On the Ridge, the fields were hilly. Some hills were too steep to plant corn or grain. If you plowed those fields, rain would wash gulleys. Those fields were the hay fields and pasture ground. Grandpa stayed on the wagon. The two boys would fork the hay onto the hay frame. Little Charlie's job was to walk around the load and tromp down the hay. It all seemed so exciting until the heat and itching got to you.

The horses went down between two windrows. The reins were tied to the front ladder. Grandpa did not have to touch the reins. He simply could direct the horses by voice. He would simply say "Molly, come around." Molly would turn and start down the next two windrows. Of course, Molly did not understand English. Grandpa said this in German. I remember giving directions in German and grandpa quickly reminded me that was his job. I remembered!

When the wagon was loaded, it was time to head for the barn. I remember the time when the wagon was loaded and the horses had to be turned up the hill with a full load of loose hay. Grandpa saw the danger. If the wagon turned on the steep hill, the load of hay might turn over. He dispatched one of his sons to go to the barn and bring back two ropes. Soon the ropes were at the wagon. They were tied to the wagon and then Norbert and Harry dug in their heels. They would keep the wagon upright. Grandpa got off the load and told Charlie to do the same. Grandpa took Molly by the rein. He spoke softly to Molly so she would not be excited. Slowly he turned the wagon with his sons pulling hard on the load. It worked! Such was the life of a hill farmer.

The load of hay is now at the barn. The wagon is parked close to the front of the barn and directly under the bonnet. The horses were unhitched. They would be harnessed to the hay fork rope to pull the hay up and into the barn.

Grandpa would drive the team; one son would stick the fork into the loose hay and one son would be in the hayloft and fork the hay after it was tripped. Charlie was to stay back and not to get close to what was going on. Those orders were strict!

When the hay was unloaded, it was not the end of the day. Everyone went back to the field to bring back another load. By the end of the day, even Charlie was tired. Norbert, Harry and grandpa were wringing wet. I itched in places I didn't know could itch. Do you know what tomorrow brought? More hay hauling!

On the Ridge, one didn't run out of work. When the day ended, there was still work to be done - cows to be milked, repairs to be made.

Courtesy of the Martin Stueve Family

SOURCES

1. Personal experience

Chapter 13
Bring Me A Cow

Waking up in the morning on the Ridge was far different then waking up in a city or town. On the Ridge, you slipped into your overalls, tied your shoes, and went to the barn lot to milk the cows. The number of cows to be milked depended usually on the number of family members to do the milking. For an individual to milk four or five cows was maximum. Let us here settle on three cows per milker. For this author on his grandfather's farm, the cows to be milked numbered nine. My two uncles milked as well as my mom and my aunt until they married. While the milking was in progress, grandpa was in the barn forking down hay for the horses. Grandma never milked. She was in the kitchen preparing breakfast.

Before the milking could begin, the cows had to be brought in from the pasture. In some cases, the cows were at the gate ready to be let into the lot. If not, they could be called in by voice. It took a loud voice. For many years, I experienced watching the family dog bring in the cows. His name was

Shep. This dog was half human. All grandpa or his sons had to do was say, "*Shep, go get them!*" and the cows fearing bite in the back of the leg, would come in quickly. It only took one bite and the cow became obedient. Shep knew not to run the cows. Of course, all commands were given to Shep in German. Shep couldn't even bark in English

An interesting thing about cows is that they always came across the field in a line and always in the same order. When I was allowed to stay at grandma and grandpa's, I wanted to bring in the cows in the evening. I was perhaps ten years old. The first time I walked up on the grazing cows I was looked at as if the cows were saying "*who's this?*". It usually took one dirt clod thrown at a cow and all of them began to move. I had strict orders not to make them run. The cows formed up walking in their predetermined order and would you believe it, in the same path. Every time it was in this order and down this path.

The milking took place in the barn lot. The milking had to be done rain or shine. If it was raining hard the cow was put in a barn stable. If the weather was bitter cold, again, the cows had to be milked. The reader should now have a basic understanding of milking. The cows had to be milked every day, twice a day, no matter what.

A particular challenge was to milk a young cow the first time. This took know how and courage. The heifer would kick and do anything but stand still. Many times, the heifer was put in a stable so it could not run and the distractions would be less. For a while there would be constant kicking of the bucket. The remedy for kicking was a pair of "kickers". This was a U-shaped clamp with a chain between the clamps. They were placed on the rear legs. When the heifer kicked it went nowhere. It also hurt. Soon the kicking stopped. After about ten days, the heifer was standing still to be milked.

At the house, grandma was cooking breakfast. Ham or bacon and eggs was often served. That together with fried potatoes, homemade bread, and jelly. If you wanted toast, you made your own. The slice of bread was buttered and laid on the hot stove top (grandma cooked on a wood range). Generally, one side was burned black. You took a table knife and scrapped off the black onto your plate.

Aumann Auctions
Lot 649 or 287
No 518 crank/cream separator

Milking is not yet finished. The full milk buckets had been brought to the house. It was now time for the cream separator. The milk was poured into the separator. This device separated the cream from the milk. The *DeLavel Separator* had to be cranked. I loved to crank, but grandpa was constantly telling me, *"not so fast!"*

The cream went into its own thirty gallon can. The other milk went back into buckets. Grandma would keep what she needed. The rest would help feed the hogs. When the cream can was full it was put on the back of the buggy and taken to the train depot in Wittenberg. The cream went by train to a creamery in St. Louis to be used to make cheese. In a few days, grandpa received a check by mail. The money would be used to purchase staples for the farm.

In the year 1945 there was a Mississippi River flood. In Illinois the farmland is flat. Cattle were in danger. The farmers in Illinois loaded their cows on barges and brought them to the Missouri side of the Mississippi River and put ashore at Star Landing. As a young boy of eight years old, I watched cattle being unloaded. Missouri farmers took the cows to their farms to milk and care for them until the river got back to normal. All the cows were marked with a metal clip in the ear as to who the owner was. My grandfather took twelve cows to his farm. His sons drove them across the roads to the Ridge. One can imagine the work strain on the family. There would also have been a lot of milk to feed the hogs and cream to sell.

Before this book leaves the milking chapter, there is a story worth telling. Young Charlie was with his parents visiting grandpa Stueve's farm on the Ridge. Charlie's dad had a day off from work on Monday. The family drove to the Ridge on a Sunday afternoon. The plan was for my dad, Norbert and Harry to go fishing on Monday and to return to Jackson (home) that evening.

It was time for the evening milking on Sunday. Grandpa, Norbert and Harry started. Then Herb, Charlie's dad, grabbed a bucket and stool to help with the milking. Charlie's mom said she would help and she took a bucket and stool. Young Charlie was not going to be left out. He was about five years old at this time. The story is that he grabbed a bucket and stool and went to the center of the barn lot. He sat down on his stool with the bucket between his legs and said, *"Bring me a cow!"*.

Today I do not remember this, but everyone in the family knows the story. Today at my house if I ask my wife to bring me something she will respond, *"bring me a cow!"*.

The hill farms at the Ridge provided strange looking cows. The pasture ground was so hilly that the cows had legs on one side that were longer than the other side so the cows could stand level when they grazed!

For a young boy, the selling of the cream was the fun part. That happened when the cream can was full. Grandpa and I would take the thirty-gallon can to the Wittenberg train depot. The system at the depot was simple. A tag was wired to the can with the creamery address and the sender's

64

address. When the train stopped at Wittenberg, the cans were loaded. The creamery would later mail a check to the sender. By the way, the four-mile trip was made using the buggy and I got to drive!

One time, the creamery advertised a special for its customers. If one would fill out a card, the sender would receive six pencils with their name on them. Grandma allowed Charlie to fill out the card. Some weeks later, six pencils arrived. On Charlie's next visit he received his pencils. The next Monday at school, this young boy was the envy of the class.

Milking was so much a part of farm life on the Ridge. It was a job to be done, done every day, and done without complaint. As often as the sun rose and set, so the milking was done.

SOURCES

1. Personal Experience

Chapter 14
Poison Ivy

How does poison ivy get into this book? Because it was everywhere. The entire United States and lower Canada has poison ivy. Another name for poison ivy is the *evil vine*.

The rest of the world is without some of America's food. They don't have turkey. Columbus said, "*it is a remarkable foul*". We have sweet corn and the potato. Ireland has potatoes but early on that was it. Later the rest of Europe was introduced to the potato. During a potato blight, Germany learned how to make an excellent whiskey out of rotten potatoes. But Europe does not know of poison ivy. The Ridge has plenty! Our country could not have grown a better crop of this vine.

The people from Hanover Germany came to the Ridge unaware. They walked through our forests. It was time for a nap on the Ridge, they laid down in the thick green ivy. They later rued the nap. A couple of days later, they woke to a rude sensation. They developed an odd, never experienced skin rash. The rash itched terribly. Their face, hands, and legs swelled. Some thought Satan himself was afflicting them. They soon learned that the beautiful lush green ivy was the source of their problem.

The early Ridge folks tried home remedies. There were purgatives and bloodletting. These brought no relief. The Indians had no cure. They were immune to poison ivy. No one died of poison ivy but it was sure aggravating.

There was an early Puritan Preacher named Cotton Mather. He said poison ivy was a tool of Satan. He said that Satan was punishing the sinfulness and worldliness of people and called for repentance. He said that since some people suffered more than others, they were more sinful.

I recall at the Ridge when my grandpa decided to clean fence rows in the fall. Everyone knows that you can tell a German's farm from the Englisher's by how clean the German's fences were. Grandpa would put on a long sleeve shirt buttoned at the collar and cuffs. His cap was pulled down tightly. At the end of the day he immediately washed with lye soap (none of the store-bought soap). This did the trick, usually! If he got poison ivy itch, grandma would find some reason why.

Remember, those people, according to Cotton Mather, that had the least immunity were guilty of the greater sins. If you were completely immune you were next to holy. I guess if you would have died from the *evil vine,* Cotton Mather would not have thought you were saved.

Grandma had a few home remedies for the terrible itch. She collected these from other people on the Ridge. The first of the home remedies was chamomile and linden blooms. These were fried in lard and used as an ointment. Lard mixed with kerosene was a favorite. Of course, if you washed with lye soap it helped. After the lye soap you were to bathe in salt water mixed with Epson Salts. Then you liberally applied vinegar. May apple roots were also good to bathe in.

Those were the days. If poison ivy would have been a cash crop, the folks on the Ridge would have been wealthy people!

SOURCES

1. The Perry County Republican, 1917

2. "That's the Way It Was", Theophil Popp, 1977

Chapter 15
MATCHES

(123rf.com)

How could matches become part of life on the Ridge? Because one match could burn down a year of work. Stick matches were a feared invention. The author learned his lesson about this instrument of destruction the hard way.

In early Ridge life, every man smoked. Most smoked a pipe. To light a pipe required a match. There were very strict rules about the use of matches on the farms on the Ridge. Never ever did you strike a match in the barn. The reason is obvious.

One of my uncles always had a pipe in his mouth. My grandpa would smoke his crooked stem pipe every evening. They both knew the rule about matches and both were faithful to obey the rules. When my uncle would near the barn he went to his favorite post near the barn lot and he laid his pipe down on top of the post. I remember seeing him do this many a time.

Where did the tobacco for the pipes come from? The people raised their own tobacco. It started with seed. It is said that the amount of seed that would fill a twenty-two cartridge would grow more tobacco than a person could smoke. Grandpa planted seeds in a small box in the house. The soil was kept moist. When a growing plant was about four to six inches tall, it was planted in an outside area where Grandpa knew the soil was rich.

The size of a grown tobacco plant is amazing. The leaves are large. At the appropriate time the leaves are cut. At the machine shed, grandpa tied the leaves into 'hands'. These were hung from the rafters in the upstairs of this shed. When it dries, they were ready to smoke in grandpa's crooked stem pipe.

Behind the heating stove was a shoe box with home grown tobacco and grandpa's pipe. Every evening, he filled his pipe and sat outside and smoked. I had an idea. I took three matches and cut off the match heads. Of course, I did not let grandma catch me. I took grandpa's pipe and filled it with tobacco. About halfway full I put in the match heads. That evening I waited for grandpa to light his pipe. He did notice that the pipe was full of tobacco but he said nothing. Outside he lit the pipe. He was enjoying his smoke. Then the fire in the pipe came to the match heads and there was a Mount Etna eruption! He held the pipe away from himself. Grandma asked *"was ist?"*. To paraphrase she asked what was going on. Grandpa said, *"I think Charlie put match heads in my pipe."* Grandma stared laughing. If not for her laughing, I think grandpa would have spanked me.

Following this came an incident that I will never forget. Let us call this *the story of the homemade pipe.* I watched the men smoke. I knew about the tobacco hanging in the machine shed. I decided I would try smoking.

I was a creative boy. Making a pipe was no problem. I cut off the end of a cane fishing pole. With a wire I cleared the center of the cane. I now had the stem for my pipe. Next, I took a corn cob and made the bowl for the pipe. I simply cut the cob and took one end and with a pocket knife hollowed out the center. Rest assured no one knew I borrowed a pocket knife. Now I had a pipe to smoke. One trip to the machine shed and I had enough tobacco to smoke.

Now, the trial of my pipe. I borrowed a couple of matches from grandpa's tobacco box. Out behind the barn I filled my pipe and began smoking. Grandpa saw the smoke. He walked up behind me and I immediately knew I was in trouble. At the house I got my spanking from grandpa. When I quit crying he put his big arm around me and said, *"Charlie, I did not spank you for smoking. I spanked you for lighting a match so close to the barn."*

I have never forgot what he said. Seventy years later I remember his words, *"never light a match near the barn!"*

The Ridge has rules and you best obey them.

SOURCES

1. Theo. Popp
2. Encyclopedia Britannica
3. Personal Experience

Chapter 16
TORNADO

Lutheran Heritage Museum, Altenburg, MO

The worst storm of all

Tri-State Tornado still holds many destructive records 90 years later

Ruins of the Longfellow School in Murphysboro, Illinois, where several children died during the Tri-State Tornado. The storm hit the school about 2:30 p.m., March 18, 1925.

Tornado

From Page 1A

TEEN INJURED IN CRASH

A 17-year-old has accident in Perry Co. 3A

A Marine's tragic death mourned in Perry. 16A

ublic MONITOR

HORROR FROM THE SKY

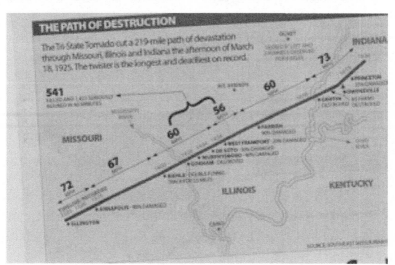

THE PATH OF DESTRUCTION

The Tri-State Tornado cut a 219-mile path of devastation through Missouri, Illinois and Indiana the afternoon of March 18, 1925. The twister is the longest and deadliest on record.

March 18, 1925 began as any other spring day on the Ridge. Everyone at the farm was up early. The cows were milked and the cream separated on the DeLavel Separator. Mom's breakfast was eggs, fried ham and homemade bread. You could have toast if you made it yourself. Either way the homemade jellies, jams, sorghum or honey was good!

March 25 was a sunny day. It was a nice day to farm. Little Ida knew she was going to have a spelling test at school. She would study the words as she walked to school.

Mom was now hoeing in the garden and Dad was sharpening sickles. Little Ida passed the spelling test. It was lunch time and Ida got her sandwich out of the lard can she used for a lunch box.

After lunch, Dad took a nap and mom put baby Harry down for a nap and went back to the garden. The clouds began to build in the sky. When dad got up from his nap, he walked to the garden and told mom he thought they were going to get a rain shower. He then left to go to the machine shed to finish the sickles.

The wind began to pick up. Mom took the dish towels off the wash line. The wind picked up and the clouds looked green. Dad came to the house. He said that he expected a strong storm.

Dad's intuition was correct. Heading for the Ridge was the most powerful tornado ever recorded. In 1925 there was no way to warn people. Today we would have ample warning of severe weather. Not in 1925. The people on the Ridge would get what they got and without warning.

The tornado first touched down about 100 miles west of Perry County. The little towns of Ellington and Annapolis were first struck. The two towns were wiped out by 2:00 P.M. This was the beginning of what would later be called the *Tri-State Tornado.* The Tri -State Tornado cut a 219-mile path of devastation through Missouri, Illinois and Indiana. This twister is the longest and deadliest on record even today.

The Stueve family was huddled in the cellar. It was mom that broke the silence and said that everyone should pray that Ida and the children in the school were safe. Little did they know what lay before this brave little girl. In the cellar was Norbert who was 6 years old and Elsie who was 3 years old. Harry was an infant about 2 months old.

The funnel cloud moved from the southeast to the northwest. The towns of Ellington and Annapolis are 20 miles apart. The storm was now moving at about 72 miles per hour. The wind was about 300 miles per hour. At Annapolis there were 200 students at school. They were unhurt. However, there were adults picked up and launched into the air. They were killed. There was a report of a baby picked up and carried 100 yards before being laid down unhurt.

The twister moved on to Leadanna (no longer in existence). Every other house was destroyed. There were 100 killed. Everyone in the town was homeless.

The tornado is now moving 67 miles per hour. It crossed Madison County and the St. Francis river valley. Two county schools were destroyed south of Fredericktown. In Madison County there were scrapes and bruises but no deaths.

This devastating storm has now traveled 50 miles in under 60 minutes. Its path is 3/4 mile wide. On the horizon is Bollinger County. The first town hit was Patton. The storm crossed Whitewater River and came to Conrad School. Oma Mayfield was teaching school that day. The school building was splintered. There were 17 children injured with none killed.

The storm continued its course. It would not relent. Next came Lixville. The tornado headed straight for Garner School House. There were 20 students preparing for a music program. The teacher yelled for the pupils to get in the center of the room. It was too late. Children were scattered. There were many hurt and unconscious. Ten-year-old Trula Henry died a week later. There were 5 deaths within 4 miles.

Next in the path was Biehle in Perry County. There were reports of flying livestock. The Catholic Church and school were hit. The church was destroyed.

This storm just will not die. It is now 80 minutes old on a run of 70 miles. A tornado is normally on the ground no more that 4 to7 miles. This storm in now moving at about 60 miles per hour. The winds are still at 300 miles per hour.

Just north of Frohna, the home of Claus Stueve was hit. It was said the house exploded. Martha Kaempfe was the sister-in-law of Claus. She was on the second floor when the house caved in. She was thrown 100 yards, breaking her neck and crushing her. She was the third Perry County death in less than 30 minutes. The wife of Claus Steve died from injuries.

This big twister is now bearing down on the Ridge. At the Ridge there were 22 students in the one room frame school house. The school house sits on the highest point of the area. Where the roads come together, there is a high knoll. At the base of the knoll is a road on the north side. The terrain slopes downhill on the north side of the road.

Little Ida was at her desk. The teacher, Irene Reents, said there would be no afternoon recess. The weather looked too bad. The wind suddenly got very still. Little Ida took notice. She sat next to Concordia Stueve. Cordie, as she was called, was Ida's cousin. Her father was Ernst Stueve the brother of Martin (Ida's father). Cordie and Ida were best friends.

Then came the roar! The door of the school house blew open. Ida and Cordie ran to the door to push it shut. Some older boys quickly pulled the piano in front of the door to keep it shut. They all succeeded but Ida later said, all of a sudden, she knew she was flying. She was up in the air and she knew it. Then the school house dropped. It was at this point Ida remembered no more.

The school house had been picked up and taken off the knoll, over the road to the north. There it was dropped. The building, with 22 pupils, was flattened. The miracle was that no one was killed. Little Ida was later found underneath the floor of the school. She was unconscious. Cordie was also badly injured.

Edmund Weber age 8 sitting on remains of Ridge School
Curtesy of the Weber Family

One would think the tornado would now give up and disappear.
Not so! The destructive force of the storm would just now begin.

From the Ridge school house to the Mississippi is about 7 miles.
The twister is still moving at about 60 miles per hour. The winds
are still 300 miles per hour.

The tornado crosses the river within minutes. Its target was
Gorham, Illinois. We now have a Bi-State tornado. Clocks in
Gorham stopped at 2:35 P.M. Five towns In Illinois were a
straight line from each other. Murphysboro was hit at 2:45 P.M.
Then came Desoto at 2:50 P.M. West Frankfurt at 3:00 P.M., and

Parish at 3:15 P.M. As it tore through these towns, it slowed to 56 miles per hour. Later it would gain speed again.

As the storm crossed the river and into Illinois, it left 11 Missourians dead and millions of dollars in property damage, dead livestock and unknown numbers of injured. However, it would be Illinois that saw the most devastation.

The tornado roared into Gorham, Illinois. Newspapers reported that Gorham was destroyed. There were 24 people killed in Gorham. Murphysboro counted 234 dead, Desoto lost 72 people of which were pupils in a school, and West Frankfort had 148 killed. Within 40 miles 541 lives were lost. When it was over, Illinois counted 606 dead. There were funerals around the clock. Some went from where they were killed straight to the cemetery.

The *St. Louis Post Dispatch* reported the next day regarding Murphysboro:

> *The whole town seemed to be on fire. The flames, leaping up in the blackened sky, made a lurid picture. We could distinguish many buildings in ruins. The headlights of a number of automobiles were turned on. The remains of one of the building and men were frantically digging in the ruins for bodies.*

The tornado which previously was the Bi-State tornado now gets the distinction of the Tri-State tornado. The twister now moved into Indiana. It struck Griffin, Owensville and Princeton. Griffin was destroyed. The area of Owensville had 85 farms destroyed. Princeton was said to have had 25 percent damage.

It was finally over. Everything about this tornado was just not believable. The average tornado lasts 13 to 20 minutes and travels 4 to 7 miles. Normally they are 400 yards wide and travel about 40 miles per hour. The time span of the Tri-State Tornado was 3 hours and 30 minutes. The travel speeds were 57 miles per hour in Missouri, 59 in Illinois and 68 miles per hour in Indiana. At its widest point it was one mile wide. The path was almost entirely straight. The entire path was 219 miles.

On March 19, the *Perry County Republican* said this:

> *Suffering and utter desolation followed in the wake of the storm, which swept down with fury upon the peaceful farming community here, leaving a trail of blood and misery and covering beautiful homes and well-equipped farms into a scene of disorder unimaginable...the wind spared few things in its path.*

One week after the tornado the *Perry County Republican* ran a headline:

Conditions Still Bad

> *While a fund of nearly a thousand dollars had been raised by businessmen of Perryville to provide food and clothing for the sufferers, and local doctors and Red Cross nurses from St. Louis have been in the field every day since the storm, the condition in dozens of homes is pitiful. With all the buildings gone with not a vestige of property except the clothing upon your back, family after family, bruised, cut, and sick, has been separated and the members are being cared for by neighbors. In several*

homes, in this and Bollinger County four or five people
are down. A dozen or more have been taken to hospitals
and several more will be sent today.

The victims are still stunned, few of the property owners
have made any headway in clearing the wreckage. So
many from families have injured members that little work
can be done toward rehabilitation of the stricken area
until wounds and fever leaves. All furniture and kitchen
utensils having vanished in the wind, housekeeping is out
of the question until new equipment is bought and some
sort of shelter erected. And in the meantime many
farmers are quartered several miles from their property.
Some are walking three- or four-miles morning and
evening to feed their stock, while many are scouting the
woods reclaiming\hay caught there by the trees.

The tornado left the Missouri hills and left for Illinois.
The flatland was perfect for a tornado. Missouri was
uneven topography. Now it was table top. Like a
steamroller it roared into Gorham. Gorham was taken by
surprise. It was a beautiful day. The recess for the
Gorham school was ended. The students took their seats
in the school. Then it got black. Totally black in the
classrooms. The building came crashing down. Mothers
ran to the school. Few children were moving. The
children were buried from elementary age to high school.
About 20 were dead.

Some students were taken to St. Louis hospitals. It was
simply a terrible situation.

It is difficult to imagine the shock and grief in all the communities, towns were simply obliterated. So many lives were lost. When the funnel cloud hit a school, children were dead in an instant. It was all instantaneous. There was no warning.

Little Ida was unconscious and under the floor of the school. Someone, and we don't know who, came across the fields to tell Martin and Caroline Stueve that their daughter was unconscious but alive. At the same time, Rudy Stueve came across the field to see about how Martin and family were. They were neighbors. Rudy had received no damage and Martin received none. Martin immediately hitched the team to the wagon. Rudy volunteered to go with him. When they arrived at the school, Martin and Rudy could not believe anyone was alive. The school house was scattered down the hillside. The two men were taken to Ida. She was not responding in spite of her dad's efforts to wake her up. Later it was determined she had received a hard blow to her forehead.

Ida was placed in the back of the wagon Martin had brought and covered with a sheet. Later in life, Ida told the story of her trip home to her daughter. She said,

> *"I was unconscious but I didn't know it. I could hear my dad and Uncle Rudy talking. When they said to put the sheet over me I thought I was dead. I do remember hearing them talk as we went home. Uncle Rudy said that he thought I would eventually die."*

Little Ida lay in bed seven days with her mother hovering over her. Every time her dad came to the house he would check on her. Then the miracle. Little Ida woke up. Her mom and dad were so relieved. There was however a problem. Ida could not talk. As hard as she would try, she couldn't say a word.

Ida's parents tried several methods to get her to talk. If she pointed to something she wanted, they would not respond hoping to get Ida to ask for it. At suppertime, if she pointed at food they wouldn't respond. Still not a sound.

Thirty days passed. If only little Ida would talk. Uncle Rudy and Uncle Ed Stueve, neighbors, came to Martin's house. They offered to take little Ida to St. Louis to be examined by an expert physician. Little Ida was examined at a hospital and the physician could find no reason why Ida was not talking. Disappointed they left for the return to Perry County.

It was not many days later Little Ida and her mom were in the chicken house gathering eggs. There was a particular chicken that always occupied a nest but never laid an egg. Ida got to that chicken. She reached under the chicken and she brought out an egg. She turned to her mom and said in German, "*the hen finally laid an egg.*" Ida's mom was in disbelief. Ida had spoken. It was over. From that day on, Little Ida jabbered continuously!

Little Ida's cousin, Cordie Stueve, was the worse hurt at the Ridge School. A piece of sheet metal cut the back of her leg. Ida said, "it cut off flesh on the back of her leg." For the rest of her life, Cordie Stueve walked with a limp.

The tornado was the topic of discussion for many years. Many pictures were taken and are available today. Newspapers carried articles about the event for several years. Nature certainly demonstrated how much power it could release.

The tornado destroyed several farms on the Ridge. However, the school was the topic of destruction. How could 22 pupils survive what took place? It was a miracle, and that miracle happened on the Ridge.

SOURCES

1. Perry County Republican

2. Southeast Missourian

3. The *St. Louis Post Dispatch*

4.   Barbara Rauh Powell, interview from Ida Stueve Rauh

Chapter 17
The Tornado
Another Source

The history of the tornado and the Ridge school that I know comes from my mother Ida Stueve Rauh. There is another recorded account of what took place when the tornado demolished the Ridge school. This account comes from Olieda Gerler Rauscher. She was in the school when the tornado carried the building and scattered it across a road and down a hill.

Olieda Rauscher later was a member of Hanover Lutheran Church in Cape Girardeau, Missouri. She told her story and experience to Elroy Kinder, a member of the church. He wrote an account of Olieda's experience. In this chapter, I have chosen to present her account exactly as Mr. Kinder wrote it.

I wish to thank Richard Weber and Mary Kiehne for sharing this account with me.

> *"Olieda", Lee's maiden name is Gerler. Her father's family has roots in Northern Germany while her mother's family, the Lichteneggers originated in Austria. She noted that there are Gerlers living south of Altenburg who were known by the location as the "lake Gerlers" since they lived near a small lake. Her family was known as the "Ridge*

*Gerlers" (Ridge, not 'rich', she says
with a smile) because of the
community in which they lived. Lee
comes from a large family, four
brothers, two living today, a sister
and a half sister, from her father's
first marriage. A brother, Edmund
Gerler lives in the Marquand
community.*

*The church building in Ridge was
used more as a school than it was for
a church. She remembers there being
only a lectern for use as a pulpit, also
the long pew type benches had a
work shelf that folded down when
schoolwork was over. In the front of
the room was the teacher's desk and
chair and chalk boards on the wall.
The brick and frame building and
playground was surrounded by six
tall trees. She remembered there
being six...or maybe it was four...The
students played baseball in among
and around the trees which were in
the way but did provide refreshing
shade on warm fall and spring days.
In 1925 the school employed a
parochial teacher for the 22 students.
The young lady stayed with the
Edmund Weber family whose home
was nearby, close enough to be*

*convenient for her to walk to and
from the classroom. The school
building faced east and the
teacherage faced towards the south.*

*The school building and its location
within the community of hard-
working families seemed to be typical
of rural Americana in the early years
of this century. The school year of
1924-1925 was about three quarters
of the way through and spring was
just around the corner. Jonquils were
beginning to bloom and occasionally
a few warm breezes would come from
the south. A few of the students would
be graduating from the eighth grade
and there was one little first grade
girl, Olieda Norma Marie Gerler,
that was having a good year.*

*All seems so typical but something
was about to happen that would
affect teacher, students, community
and people in parts of three states for
the rest of their lives, for some, into
the next century which at that time
seemed so remote.*

*March 18, 1925 began much like
other days for Lee and her brothers
and sisters. They dressed, had*

breakfast, gathered their books, pencil boxes and lunch pails and headed for the school house. They had about one-half mile to walk but the early spring day was clear and pleasantly warm. After arriving at school, the session of "books" began with each grade level being called upon for recitation, then seat work while other grades were given attention by the lone teacher.

As the day progressed, time for lunch and playground games passed and the early afternoon studies began. Some may have noticed the clouds that were forming on the western horizon toward the Biehle and Apple Creek direction. The gentle breeze became noticeably more intense and the sky was becoming overcast which caused the school room to be almost too dark for work. Schoolwork continued but a whispered "It's a storm a coming up," caused most in the room to glance towards the windows and the darkening sky. Suddenly a violent gust of wind cast open the front door. The teacher asked on the girls near the back to please go close the door. She pushed the door shut and returned to her seat. Again, the door was cast open by a violent wind gust! "Please go and close the door again," the teacher instructed the girl in the back. The door was pushed shut and the latch was secured. The wind outside was now blowing with an awful force, bending the tree limbs almost to the ground, and causing some to swish against the front windows. The door latch could not withstand the mounting force and came open once again filling the room with scattered papers. The teacher asked all the children to move to the door and hold it shut. As they were gathered to secure the door, three limbs crashed against the front window panes breaking the glass and part of tree limbs came through into the room! Looking out the window they could see a mass of thick, dark fog rolling over the hills, coming in the direction of the school - "Like a huge column of very black coal smoke, nearly a mile wide" as described later by one witness in the community. The Students and teacher now were aware that this was not going to be an ordinary storm, with all the wind, rain and mounting damage around them. Several of the students began crying as they feared for their safety.

Lee remembers vividly the event up to that time. Now she felt the entire school room begin to tremble and shake causing her to fall between two of the long pew-desks. She remembers hitting the floor and feeling something terribly heavy strike her in her back. She then remembers nothing until awakening outside amid a deluge of rainfall with lightning and thundering a gale force wind.

Unknown to her at the time was the extent of the damage to the school. As she later was told, the force of the wind, now know to be violent tornado, had lifted the frame school building and with its precious "cargo" of 22 terrified students and teacher clearing the surrounding tree tops and came to a landing several yards to the east of its original location. There was nothing left of the framing, it was in total pieces except for the floor and the floor joists which had fluttered upside down on-air currents, dropping gently enough that those it covered

*were not crushed. The roof was found
in pieces many yards away.
Amazingly the trees were not severely
damaged, losing only most of their
leaves and a few smaller limbs. Lee
describes the school house a "coming
down in a million pieces." The
teacher and many of the students
were found huddled in one location,
others had been scattered as the
building was lifted and came apart in
the air, then strewn down the hillside.
However, all were safe with some
bruises and a few bone fractures. It
was raining, "in sheets," Lee
describes as she remembers lying
amidst the rubble of the building.
One of the girls she believes it was
Elda Engert, came near her and Lee
grabbed hold of her dress tail. Elda
helped her up and with other girls
they all held hands in the driving rain
and made their way to the Edmund
Weber house. Arriving at the house
they saw that it had been moved a
few feet off its foundation and the
cellar could be seen. Lee almost fell
into the open cellar but somebody
grabbed her and they proceeded into
the house. She remembers leaning
over something to ease the pain in*

*her back caused by the object that fell
on her.*

*Soon the wind died down, the rain
began to slow and the clouds became
lighter and broken. The community
slowly learned the terrifying news
that the path of the tornado, so very
clear through the community, had
squarely hit the school. There must
have been moments of numbing fear
for the safety of their children after
seeing the total destruction of the
building. Lee's Dad and her brother
Roland came to the door of the
teacherage and found her, safe but
certainly scared and barely able to
walk. They started towards home and
because of the pain she was unable to
cross a rail fence and had to be
helped by her big brother.*

*The injury to her back has caused her
discomfort all her life and certainly is
a constant reminder of the day the
Hand of God reached down, gathered
those children and their teacher
together, and spared them from the
wrath of the March 18, 1925 tornado.
Leaving Missouri, the strange cloud
appeared to be breaking up in the
Mississippi River bottoms. The black*

*fog began dissipating and unveiled
twin funnels moving side-by-side.
Plowing across the water, the storm
shrouded itself in fog again and
headed for the Illinois towns of
Gorham and Murphysboro, DeSoto
and West Frankfort. These towns
sustained severe damage and much
loss of life with DeSoto almost being
wiped from the map!*

*No one from the Ridge School died,
and only a few debilitating injuries
would last among the students from
that terrifying afternoon. This
extraordinary case of schoolhouse
survivors at Ridge and several other
schools from Annapolis, Missouri
into Indiana, will always be cited in
studies on tornadoes."*

The fact that no one died is truly remarkable. In Illinois,
hundreds of children died as a result of this tornado. Those
children for the most part were in brick buildings. Here on the
Ridge we have a frame building. When it was over there was no
boards still nailed to another. The story of this tornado has
passed into history. It needs to be told again and remembered
how the Lord spared the lives of this small group of children.

SOURCES

1. Olieda Gerler Raucher, by Elroy Kinder

Chapter 18
THE JUDGE

Edward Bernhard Leimbach was born on April 7, 1876. He was
the second child born to Ernst and Anna Holschen Leimbach.
We here notice the names of Leimbach and Holschen. There
were, in the early days, steamboat landings on the Mississippi
River, Two landings with these names. There was Holschen
Landing which eventually became known as Star Landing and
there was Leimbach Landing. From maps of that time we know
the exact location of these landings.

Edward's father was Ernst August Leimbach. From early records
it appears he served on the Federal side during the Civil War.

Nothing is known about Edward's early years on the farm. This
we know, the farm was isolated on the second ridge adjacent to
the Mississippi river. In fact, from certain points on the property
you could look across the river and see Jacob, Illinois.

By the time he was nine-teen (19) years old, he was no longer on
the Ridge. He was working on a farm in Iowa. Again, we know
no details of why this took place. We only speculate that the
family could not afford raising and feeding a child so young
Edward left home. There is a document which gives us a small
amount of information. He worked as a farm hand and received
no compensation, this probably means he worked for room and
board only.

After two years Edward was back home in Perry County. At the
age of 19 he registered for the draft. His draft registration is in

the possession of Warren Schmidt. Warren Schmidt volunteers at the Lutheran Heritage Museum in Altenburg, Missouri. Edward served during World War I. Before leaving for the army he married Frieda Holschen. Edward left for service six months later. His wife was pregnant. The child Emilie, was born in November 1918. While Frieda was giving birth, Edward was at Camp Dodge, Iowa. He did not go overseas.

Sometime during the early life, Edward Leimbach became known as Ed. From this point on, we will call him Ed. By the year 1922, Ed is twenty-six years old. He is farming on the Ridge. 1922 was a year of dramatic events. First there was the train wreck at Star Landing. Then came the train robbery which ended with two bandits being shot and killed at Wittenberg (read *The Train Robber* by this author). There must have been plenty to talk about.

Then came 1925. That is the year of the tornado. The Leimbach farm was hard hit as was the Holschen farm. Photos exist today of the damage to both these properties. Leimbach was a determined man. He now had two children ages seven and five. He built all the building back.

Ed next invested in a threshing machine and steam engine. He was the center of the Ridge threshing ring. I remember being part of and seeing him thresh Martin Stueve's crops.

Ed lost most of his hand in an accident. Leo Steffens thinks it was in a corn shredder. He had only an index finger left on the hand.

Today Perry County has County Commissioners who see to the affairs of the county. In the earlier times they were called Judges. Ed Leimbach was elected to be a County Judge. For many years he was called Judge Leimbach. He was a very respected man at the courthouse in Perryville. I learned that later he was elected Presiding Judge for Perry County. Ed died in 1985. His wife Frieda died in 1976. Both are buried in Immanuel Lutheran Church cemetery in Altenburg, Missouri.

SOURCES

1. Lutheran Heritage Center and Museum, Blog posted by Warren Schmidt.

Chapter 19
STAR LANDING

Photos courtesy of the Lutheran Heritage Museum, Altenburg, Missouri

Tucked away in a small area of the Ridge was a boat landing. The landing was north of the second Ridge. Unless one wanted to go to the landing, one would never find it accidently. Yet, in the area were many small farms. Saxons were settling the area. There was a need for a landing so farmers could receive goods and for these farmers to ship livestock to the St. Louis stockyard.

When one reads the history of the Saxon immigration in 1839, the reader will find the names of all the immigrants and their occupations in Germany. There are linen weavers, cobblers, hatters, farmers and many other occupations. Nowhere does one find a sheepherder. In 1872, Daniel Wichern immigrated to America and listed his occupation as a sheepherder. He was eighteen years old when he immigrated.

Young Daniel Wichern found employment work at DeLassus Drug Store at Red Rock Landing (near Crosstown and Farrar). The store was owned by a Mr. DeLassus. As was the case of all the river towns, flooding was a constant problem. Daniel decided to open his own business. He traveled down river and came to what we now know as Star Landing.

Daniel Wichern purchased five acres of ground from Louis Holschen in 1889. He first constructed a home and then a store. He named his area Star Landing.

A trip to the site of Star Landing will convince anyone that farming in the immediate area would be impossible. The terrain offers nothing but hills and steep hills at that. Daniel Wichern looked across the river and saw nothing but flat land. Between Daniel and Illinois was a small island suitable for farming.

Daniel rented this island from a Mr. Amschler and began farming the ground.

To become eligible for citizenship one needed to register at the court house in Perryville, Missouri. One also named two witnesses that would say you were of good character. Daniel appeared on the appointed date. For some reason his witnesses did not appear. The citizenship hearing was rescheduled. At the next hearing the witness again failed to appear. The third time Daniel appeared the witnesses also appeared. On April 15, 1913, Daniel Wichern became a citizen of the United States of America.

Daniel Wichern prospered with his store and farming operation. The store was on the river side of the tracks and the house on the other side. People in the Ridge area came to his store to purchase goods. The store was of the mercantile type. One could purchase groceries, nails, clothing, needles and thread and most everything. Mrs. Wichern was also known to advertise in the *Perry County* newspaper.

Daniel had a ewe that gave birth to triplets. He gave one of the lambs to his daughter Mildred. She raised the lamb on a bottle. The lamb became very attached to her following her wherever she went. She had to be careful the lamb didn't follow her to school. Get it?
In 1922, Daniel Wichern's home burned. Daniel was on Amschler island with his sons tending cattle when they saw smoke at the landing. He built a new home on the same location. To compound the problem he faced, the store was flooded due to the rising Mississippi River. The river almost

destroyed the store. Daniel and his sons rebuilt the store on the other side of the tracks.

Daniel Wichern would not be dissuaded. He and his sons tore down the store. The lumber was used to add to his home and he operated his store as a part of the house.

The boat landing brought much business to Wichern's store. A great many cows, steers, hogs and chickens were shipped to the St. Louis Markets.

Stories are told about Daniel Wichern and his case of liquor. He worked with Slim Killion from Gorham, Illinois. Dan would furnish the sugar and Slim made booze. Slim had to avoid the Revenue Agents who knew he was selling liquor. To escape he once jumped into the Mississippi River and swam to Missouri. Once he was caught but Daniel bailed him out of jail.

Daniel Wichern was an entrepreneur. The property for his boat landing was purchased from John Swan. He also operated a ferry to take people back and forth between Missouri and Illinois. On the Illinois side of the River he used Estel Landing. The ferry operated between 1895 and 1899. Leo Steffens remembers he and his brother taking the ferry to Illinois many times.

Daniel Wichern passed away in 1942. The store and boat landing closed. The contents of the store were purchased by Fisher Store in Altenburg.

History does not remember Daniel Wichern. It should! From the time of his arrival in American in 1872 until his death in 1942

Daniel Wichern left his mark. He no doubt worked hard. He was a visionary. He saw a need and he set out to satisfy a need. He bought and sold goods, farmed and provided needed transportation across the Mississippi River and back. To accomplish what he did sets him apart from others. He took his ideas, his ambitions and his passions to succeed in American to a higher level.

Star Landing became a focus of attention in September, 1922. The headline in the local newspaper read:

2 KILLED AND 32 INJURED IN WRECK NEAR SEVENTY-SIX

Photo courtesy of the Lutheran Heritage Museum, Altenburg, MO

The train wreck was at Star Landing. The Frisco Train number 805 crashed at 4 o'clock in the morning. The Frisco train was the victim of a collapsed train trestle. The trestle or bridge was washed out during a heavy rain. The accident happened at about two miles south of Seventy-Six, Missouri.

During a very heavy rain, which the newspaper called a cloud burst, the trestle was weakened. Residents of the Star Landing area told the newspaper that it was generally known that all the trestles in the area were not in good condition. They all reported that there were rotting timbers under the trestles. They also said that the supporting pilings were rotting. The roaring water came down the creek and caused the trestle to give way.

When the accident took place, the train was traveling at about thirty-five miles per hour. When the train approached the trestle the locomotive and baggage car made it across. When a second baggage car was on the trestle, it gave way. The second baggage car nosed into the bank. This caused the locomotive and first baggage car to overturn.
 Into the space left by the second baggage car came the mail car which crashed into the empty space. Next came what was called a chair car and it went on top of what was before it. This car was made of steel which prevented a great loss of life. The rear half of the train consisted of a club car and three sleeper cars. These remained on the rails said the newspapers.

The engineer and fireman were in the locomotive and were thrown clear when the locomotive overturned. Neither was seriously injured. The conductor and a negro porter were unhurt. They had both been in a wreck at Horin the week before. To survive two train wrecks was a miracle in 1922.

The newspaper reported that J. T. Warmath from Gibson City, Tennessee was killed. His head was crushed. The newspaper said he was carrying a $400.00 check which was in his coat pocket. The other person killed was S. M. Yearta of Hayti, Missouri. He was sixteen years old.

It took quite a period of time to clean up the mess left by the train wreck. Cranes to lift the cars were brought in. It was weeks before normal train travel was restored. There was also now pressure on the Frisco to assure all their trestles were safe, even in inclement weather.

The reader is reminded that in November of 1922 that the Frisco was robbed and the two robbers were shot and killed in Wittenberg. The area had all the news and excitement that it needed.

Daniel Wichern was not a church going man but he was a Christian. He once said that he had read the Bible ten times from cover to cover. When he was with a pastor he loved to ask him questions to stump him. The story is told that he was rowing a pastor across the river. The boat started leaking. The pastor started praying. Daniel was to have said, "*Pastor, there is a time for praying and a time to dip water. Now you dip and I'll row and we will do just fine.*" Daniel had a housekeeper that regularly went to church. Daniel would have her preach the pastor's sermon to him.

In the 1930's Daniel Wichern became acquainted with a young preacher from Germany. He convinced Daniel to start going to church. Daniel Wichern regularly went to church until he died.

The history of Star Landing has passed into history no longer remembered. The store owned by Daniel Wichern is forgotten. So are the events of the train wreck and the train robbery. But the history is real and it really took place at a lonesome place called the Ridge.

Claus   Grandpa Dan   Grandma holding Clara
                    Emma   house up on the hill
Bill (William)   Charles   behind the store

Daniel & Maria Wichern Family abt 1897

Photo courtesy of Diane Wunderlich

Photo courtesy of Diane Wunderlich

Photo courtesy of Diane Wunderlich

Photos curtesy of Diane Wunderlich

SOURCES

1. Facts on Daniel Wichern, Mildred Kranawetter.

2. Ibid

3. Ibid

4. Ibid

Chapter 20
Mack's Chapel

During the early years of the Ridge there was a significant population of African Americans that owned ground, farmed and worked in the community as general laborers. Where do they live and where did they come from? One hasn't done his homework if he simply says, "they were always there".

It all goes back to slave ownership in Perry County. This leads to the question, "how much we know about slavery in Perry county?' We know a lot. There were two priests assigned to Ste. Marys Seminary in Perryville. These two priests decided to write a history of the slaves. If you wish to read their account the book can be reviewed at the Perry County Historical Society.

During the days of slavery, a person had to declare to the county how many slaves he owned, how old they were and their names. Slaves were a taxable asset. The two priests were able to record an accurate history of slaves in Perry County even to drawing a map of Perry County with the location of slave owners and the number of slaves owned.

With this background, I will recall a little known and forgotten piece of the history of the Ridge. There was a significant population of blacks living on the Ridge. These African Americans had their own church called Mack's Chapel and they operated a school called Lincoln School.

During the year 2015, Richard Young thoroughly researched the history of black people on the Ridge. It is from his research that much of what follows has been drawn. Also, I personally interviewed Leo Steffens asking him to recall life on the Ridge.

Mr. Young tells us at the beginning of his research paper that his interest peaked regarding this back community when he visited the cemetery of Mack's Chapel. This took place at the encouragement of Dorothy Weinhold a docent at the Lutheran Heritage Center in Altenburg. In Young's first visit to the site of Mack's Chapel he found a tombstone in the cemetery belonging to Eliza Buford who died in 1894.

How did a black community emerge in Perry County this early in History? Where did these African-Americans come from?

How did they sustain themselves? Did they mesh into the white-German community?

Let us begin to answer these questions with a quote from Richard Young:

> ...in the years following the American Civil War, a small But vibrant community of freed blacks flourished, for a time in the rocky hills adjacent to the Mississippi River. Here, literally surrounded by the dominant white culture of former slave owners, Lutheran and Presbyterian farmers and merchants, freed slaves and their children sank roots in the soil of southeastern Perry County. ₁

These blacks borrowed money and purchased small tracts of land. They borrowed their money from the Bank of Altenburg. In those early years following the Civil War, land was available for five dollars an acre. The people also established their own school called by many, *the Colored School.*

The two Priests from St. Marys Seminary established the slave population in Perry County at 765 blacks. The slaves living in the Seventy-Six area, Brazeau Township, numbered 281.

For the reader not familiar with Perry County, the Ridge and Seventy-Six, the following might help. Seventy-Six was founded by John Wilkinson. It was located on the bank of the Mississippi River. It is a part of the Brazeau township and is a stone's throw from the Rudy Steffens farm and orchard located on the Ridge.

This John Wilkinson was known to be the wealthiest person in Perry County. He operated an orchard. He had three slaves. Following emancipation, he hired numerous blacks to work in the orchard. The black community of Mack's Chapel would have been next door. When Wilkerson died, he owned eleven thousand acres in Missouri, Texas and Illinois.

Wilkinson's orchard provided plenty of work for the black community. It is recorded that he had 1000 trees in his orchard. The *Perry County Sun* reported that Wilkinson employed twenty men in his orchard. 2

The first land owner in this black community was William Burford. He received his land from his slave owner in consideration of his valuable service. 3

A family named Hughey sold several small tracts of land to blacks. 4

The cemetery at Mack's Chapel is now invisible. It is overgrown by vegetation. A careful search will reveal several stones with names and many graves marked by a plain stone. There are over forty graves marked. All graves face east. 5

The earliest burial was that of William Bufford in 1892. The last is that of Paris Pringle in 1934. The oldest person buried in the cemetery is Charles Davis who was 102 years old when he died. 6

The cemetery at Mack's Chapel has had several names over the years. It was known as the Colored Baptist Cemetery, Mack's

Chapel, Mike's Chapel, Mc's Chapel, Seventy-Six cemetery and the Seventy-Six Colored Cemetery.

There was a personality living in the black community who needs to be remembered. He was the oldest person buried at Mack's Chapel. He was Charles Davis or known as Happy Davis. He was born in 1840. When the Civil War began he was twenty years old. He is remembered by Leo and Herb Steffens as a man who was always laughing. He played a banjo and was literally "egged" out of Perryville because on of his performances go to boisterous. This was reported by *The Perry County Republican*. At the East Perry County Fair, he sat on a wall and played his banjo. He had a hat laying beside him to gather coins from anyone who liked his music.

There was a William Sims, a negro, that began his own business. He bought a row boat and began a ferry service for people wanting to go to Illinois. The fee to cross the river was fifty-cents. Leo Steffens remembers having Sims row him across the river. 7

It is believed that Sims was the last funeral at Mack's Chapel. The day of his funeral was a rainy day. To get Sims to the cemetery, the Steffens family offered the use of their tractor. 8

In his paper on Mack's Chapel, Mr. Young gives insight into the beginning of Mack's Chapel. Young quotes Dorothy Weinhold of this matter. Originally, the church was called Ridge Chapel. The church was built, according to Weinhold, in about 1918 on a site donated by a member of the black community. 9

Today there is nothing left of Mack's Chapel. The ground is covered by vegetation. All that remains is the cornerstone. It may be seen at the Lutheran Heritage Center and Museum in Altenburg, Missouri. The stone measures two-feet wide, two and a half feet long, and four inches thick. The following appears on the face of the stone:

MACK'S
Chapel Church
1921

DEACONS

A. Bufford	Levi Beal
W. Sims	Chas Davis
L. Pringle	C. Gillwater
W. Abbot	
A. Mattingly	

Levi Beal	CLERK
W. JONES	PASTOR 10

Was Mack's Chapel the only building used for worship? Young indicates that it was not. In an interview with Herb and Leo Steffens, he says the Steffens remember a building west of Mack's Chapel. It was a room and built of logs. This building was first used according to the Steffens as "the colored school." The original purpose of the building was for worship. 11

There is a discrepancy regarding the first Pastor. The cornerstone says W. Jones. Leo and Herb Steffens recall that Levi Beal was the pastor in the 1920's. 12

Mack's Chapel frequently conducted baptisms on the Steffens Farm. There was a pond that was used. The Steffens boys would chase cattle from the pond so a baptism could proceed. 13

About the time of World War II, Mack's Chapel closed. The people moved away. The elderly died and a piece of Ridge history died with them.

We shall now consider the history of the "colored school" in the Mack's Chapel Community. It needs remembering that the education of blacks was illegal prior to the Civil War. By the 1900's blacks were being eligible for education. Progress was very slow. The black community wanted their children to receive an education. The children wanted to learn to read and write.

Perry County was very active in beginning schools. Records show that in 1904-1905 there were fifty-eight schools in Perry County. There was one school called a "colored school." That school was located in Seventy-Six. The land for the school was donated by George Hatch.

George Hatch
Courtesy of Lutheran Heritage Center & Museum

Chapter 21
SEVENTY-SIX

Who would name a town Seventy-Six? John Wilkinson thought it was an appropriate name. Why? Who knows!

In this book and especially in describing events surrounding Mack's Chapel mention has been made of the town of Seventy-Six. While the town is not on the Ridge, it is barely down the hill from the Ridge and Steffen's Orchard. The town of Seventy-Six sits on the bank of the Mississippi River. The train goes through the town and right smack dab through the middle of the town. The town deserves mentioning. It may not have been on the Ridge, but people from the Ridge and Seventy-Six reach out and shake hands with one another.

Where did it get its name? There are three theories. You can pick the reason you like because no one knows where the name Seventy-Six came from.

> It got its name because it was the 76th boat landing south of St. Louis.

> It was the 76th birthday of John Wilkinson when he named the town.

> Wilkinson had made 75 successful boat landings and it was here he sank his boat.

John Wilkinson
Courtesy of Lutheran Heritage Center & Museum

Whichever you choose, John Wilkinson painted a sign and put it up next to the river "76 LDG." It stuck. The town had a name when he made application for a post office. That document does not include a hyphen in the word Seventy-Six.

John Wilkinson came to the United States from Yorkshire, England. He arrived with his parents in the year 1816, at the age of three years old. At the age of sixteen, he became an apprentice in the ship building trade. In 1835, he invested in his own ship. His ship was the *Laurel*. The ship sunk two miles north of what would become Seventy-Six. He began to forge a living with the clothes on his back. He would end up the wealthiest man in Missouri.

John Wilkinson took the wreckage from his ship and built a shanty to live in. He immediately became a dealer selling cord wood. Wood was the fuel for river boats. He sold his wood to river men.

In the winter he brought his wood to the river using a hand sled. In the summer he used a wheelbarrow. Later he conceived the idea of loading the wood on flat boats which the upstream traffic could pick up without making a stop. After unloading, his flatboat was set adrift and he would snag them. He worked this way until he was able to buy a team of oxen. Business became so good, he employed forty to fifty men. Many of these were blacks from the Mack's Chapel area.

When Wilkinson accumulated surplus money, he invested in buying land. At one time he owned 120,000 acres and was the largest taxpayer in Perry County. He bought a 1600-acre island in the Mississippi river called Wilkinson's Island. He also acquired land in Illinois and Texas.

John Wilkinson had the largest cord wood business on the river. He invented the circular saw and he erected a water powered mill near Altenburg on Apple Creek. He had a large family but only three children survived him.

In 1860, Wilkinson constructed a very large home in Seventy-Six. On the front of the house were six columns. The front doors were made of black walnut. This was said to be the most beautiful house on the Mississippi River.

John Wilkinson died in 1876. On top of a bluff overlooking the river he was buried. In 1934, the beautiful home burned.

Next to come to Seventy-Six was George Hatch. George Hatch took all the acreage where Wilkinson had removed trees and began an orchard. He powered the fruit industry in Southeast Missouri. He built a general store and a tavern. The saloon was near the river bank. The soil eroded and the saloon slipped into the river. The town had a dress shop and hat shop. From miles around people came to Seventy-Six to visit the post office. Hatch opened a hotel to be used by train crews. It was the orchard that provided many jobs for people in the area. The blacks from Mack's Chapel found much work at Hatch's Orchard.

It was at Seventy-Six that the train robber Jack Kennedy and his partner William Logsdon boarded the Frisco train and robbed the express car. The robbery happened in 1922. Both men were shot and killed by a posse of eleven men at Wittenberg, Missouri.

Wittenberg grew and Seventy-Six declined. Today the town is a ghost town. All that is left is owned by the Missouri Conservation Department. Such is history.

Hatch came to the area from the East Coast. He married into the Wilkinson family. Wilkinson was the founder of Seventy-Six. He was able to acquire land and he began an orchard in the area. Many blacks worked in his orchards. 12

A school was established. The school was called Union School. There was a separate building for blacks. No records exist for the black school. 15

Richard Young interviewed Herb and Leo Steffens regarding the beginning of the black school in the Mack's Chapel area. They recall two successive buildings in the area. The first was just south of Mack's Chapel on the western side of the cemetery. It was one room with a gable roof. This school may have served at the first church. 17

According to the Steffens, the "second colored school" at Seventy-Six was located on the Finger property near Union School. This would have been adjacent to Mack's Chapel. This school survived and served the community for many years. 18

Young says, "with the decline in enrollment of African American students that occurred during the early 1940's, it is apparent the "second colored school" served the needs of a rapidly declining population. Since the new school site was less isolated than the original school building, it may also have been easier for the remaining students to reach their classroom. 19

Who paid for the education of the black students? There are existing records for the accounting of money and the number of students. The highest counts happened between the years 1895 to 1902. The count ranged from 10 to twelve students. In 1893, there were ninety-six (96) white students in the Brazeau township. The state of Missouri allocated $1.82 and $0.09 per child in 1911. The township allocated $0.29 for African-American students. Believe it or not, whites and blacks received the same amount. During the 1927-1928 school year there were twenty (20) pupils in the "colored school." 20

The school at Mack's Chapel eventually became known as Lincoln School.

Dorothy Weinhold recalls that in the 1930's, the residents of Mack's Chapel were seldom seen. They would be occasionally seen in Frohna buying goods. To the Frohna children the sight of black people was something to be noticed. 23

Beginning in 1919, the District assigned teachers to the school. One of the first assigned teachers was Eva Rowan. She taught one year. Rowan married Philip Burford in 1921. The marriage ceremony was performed by Pastor Vogel in Altenburg.

In the years 1926-1927, Shannon Eulingberg taught school. The Author personally knew Mr. Eulingberg. In later years, he owned and operated a small store just south of Old Appleton on highway 61. It is thought that Shannon Eulingberg came to Mack's Chapel from Old Appleton. 21

Accurate records exit of the names of black students a Mack's Chapel. The list of students begins in 1910-1922. The first student listed is Arthur Beal age 18. The last enrollment was in 1945-`1946. The students were Rosa Hull and Lloyd Barber. 22

During the early years of Perryville, the blacks did not often visit this town. It was a "sundown" town. All blacks had the be out of town by sundown. The blacks from St. Mary also avoided Perryville. 23

History recalls a tragic event in the Mack's Chapel area. Leo Steffens recalls the accident that occurred with fourteen (14) year old Pearl Farrar. Pearl was a boy. Farrar an African-American was mistaken for a possum and shot out of a tree with a shot gun. The boy was hit in the head and died instantly. The accident took place on October 28, 1916.
The Perry County Republican reported the accident. The newspaper said:

> 'Pearl Farrar, a thirteen-year-old colored boy,
> was accidently Killed by a shotgun in the hands
> of Henry Frentzel, a son of A.A. Frentzel of
> Uniontown, last Saturday night. Squire Amschler
> of Uniontown summoned a jury and had an inquest.
> The verdict was that the boy had come to his death
> by a shotgun wound to the head." 24

Another incident appeared in the *Perry County Sun* May 21, 1875. A child, the son of Charles Barber was killed. He died as the result of injuries when the wind blew one of the house doors upon him.

The *Perry County Republican* reported "a colored couple from Seventy-Six called on Rev. Vogel (Altenburg) Sunday and had him tie the knot which made them one." 26

Finally, the *Perry County Republican* reported Herman Levi Barber and Ecarer Albert Barber for conducting an illegal "crap game" at Old Appleton. 27

There are in the Perry County Courthouse rather complete records of people living on the Ridge. The reader might also go to The Lutheran Heritage Center in Altenburg and read Richard Young's Paper on Mack's Chapel. He gave us an excellent summary. 28

How could it be that a community of African Americans came to live and settle on the Ridge? It happened because former slaves from the area decided not to leave. They survived because as slaves they had learned to farm the hills of the Ridge. They also found work in the Hatch Orchard in Seventy-Six. They also found day work in the immediate area. The former slaves cut much firewood to be sold to steamboats traveling the river.

The former slaves living on the Ridge had learned the Christian religion from their owners. They built a school for their children first and then a church. Religion was important to these blacks. To build a school and church to a lot of working together. It would have been expensive requiring all to contribute. They contributed money and hard work.

The maximum enrollment was twenty-three in 1931. In 1946 there were only two. For ninety-five years education and the Christian faith were the center of the community. 29

The federal census in 1870 shows fifty blacks on the Ridge. The years around the 1870s show that there were eighty or more blacks on the Ridge. It was in the 1900s that the population began to decline. In 1947, there was no longer a school. 30

Mack's Chapel is certainly interesting history and important history. If the history of Mack's Chapel was not written, an important part of the Ridge history would leave a void. The community of blacks lived peaceable among a white German population. One has to commend the Steffens family. They no doubt provided a lot of friendship and aid to the Mack's Capel community.

Mack's Chapel…it's real history and important history of the Ridge.

SOURCES

1. Mack's Chapel, and the African American Community of Seventy-Six, Missouri, Richard Young.

2. The *Perry County Sun,* October 12, 1899.

3. Mack's Chapel, and the African American Community of Seventy-Six, Missouri, Richard Young.

4. Ibid

5. Ibid

6. Ibid

7. Interview, Leo Steffens

8. Ibid

9. Mack's Chapel, and the African American Community of Seventy-Six, Missouri, Richard Young.

10 - 30. Ibid

NOTE: for more information on Mack's Chapel, see the book by the same name, written by this author.

Note: Photos in this chapter are courtesy of Lutheran Heritage Center & Museum

Chapter 22
STEFFEN'S ORCHARD

(Noenning Orchard)
**(Courtesy of Lutheran Heritage Museum, Altenburg,
Missouri)**

Many people have heard of Steffen's Orchard. Not many people know the size and scope of this orchard. At its peak Steffen's Orchard was a sizeable operation. Rudy Steffens was one who emerged on the Ridge as a businessman who knew how to grow and expand a business.

The example Rudy Steffens had of beginning an orchard, he no doubt learned by being aware of G.S. Hatch Orchard in Seventy-Six, Missouri. That orchard would have been next door to the

Steffens' farm at the Ridge. Hatch operated a large orchard utilizing African-American labor from the Mack's Chapel area. Hatch sold his fruit to the population in East Perry County and he shipped his goods to St. Louis using both the railroad and steamboats.

As has been described in this book, a church named Mack's Chapel abutted to the Steffens' property. Rudy had inherited his farm from his father Claus Steffens who immigrated to America in 1871. Leo Steffens says Rudy's father was not nearly as aggressive in business as Rudy became.

The black Community at Mack's Chapel began to disintegrate. As they left the Ridge, Rudy would purchase their small tracts of land which ranged from twenty acres to fifty acres. With the departure of the blacks, Rudy's farm grew to 365 acres.

An Altenburg landmark is the Steffens fruit stand at the intersection of State Roads C and A. For many years this was the place where people came from miles around to purchase apples and peaches. Not only could you purchase your fruit in Altenburg, the Steffens family also sold their fruit in Jackson, Perryville, Chester, Illinois and St. Louis, Missouri. This was a sizeable business operation. How did this large fruit business find itself on the Ridge in Perry County?

It begins with the immigration of Claus Steffens. Claus was born in 1854. In 1871 he left Hanover, Germany and traveled to the United States. He knew of others who were settling in Perry County in Missouri and especially the Ridge community. In a remote corner of the Ridge he purchased his land to begin a farming operation. As has been written previously in this book the farm was adjacent to Mack's Chapel and the black community on the Ridge.

Claus Steffens farmed and raised a family. The children attended the Ridge School. One of the children of Claus was Rudy. Rudy was an aggressive and ambitious man. He had to have known the success of George Hatch and his orchard at Seventy-Six. Hatch sold apples and peaches to people far and wide.

Meanwhile the black community at Mack's Chapel was beginning to sell their plots of ground and moving to other places. As a plot came up for sale Rudy Steffens bought it. His farm grew to 365 acres. There was enough ground to begin an orchard.

Rudy Steffens planted 300 apple trees in 1925. The trees grew well so Rudy began the next step. He planted peach trees. To say the orchard blossomed would be a play on words, but that was the case. Rudy began selling his fruit to people who came to his far. He also had an "apple route" in Perryville.

Rudy Steffens was an astute businessman. He needed a more efficient outlet for his fruit. He purchased an old house in Altenburg. On the lot he built a fruit stand. Apples and peaches were hauled to the stand by the truck load. People needed not to drive to the Ridge to purchase apples, they were now in Altenburg. The fruit business grew and grew. More trees were being planted. As these began to produce even more trees were planted. In 1960 the Altenburg fruit stand was enlarged.

Rudy's brother, Ferdinand, also tried his hand at the orchard business. He, however, did not grow his orchard to the extent of Rudy's orchard.

Rudy Steffens grew a variety of apples. There was the Golden Delicious and the Red Delicious. However, the Jonathan variety was the top seller. These trees had to be pruned each year and each tree sprayed with an insecticide. The orchard business was a lot of hard work. Also, the rest of the farm had to be plowed and cultivated. Rudy's two sons, Herb and Willard had few days off from work. If it wasn't the orchard then it was the farm. When the farm work was caught up then it was back to the orchard.

When it was time to pick peaches or apples the entire family got involved. Everyone picked apples. The apples went into bushel baskets. If you called ahead you could pick up your bushel of apples when you went to the East Perry County Fair. Your name would be on a slip of paper inserted into the apples. The system worked and worked well.

Not content with peaches and apples the Steffens sons began to grow plum, cherry, nectarine and apricot trees. Herb and Willard continued to grow the orchard business. These two had an opportunity to further grow the business. These fruits in Altenburg were for sale. The sons bought the orchard. The distribution got even larger.

Today when you drive through Altenburg you can still see the Steffens Orchard fruit stand. It stands as a reminder of hard work, ingenuity and vision. Rudy Steffens was all of this. His sons continued the vision. There never was any fanfare about the Steffens Orchard operation. All just admired their hard work. Today it is only a memory. At one time there were 5400 fruit trees growing and producing on the Ridge. Wow!

SOURCES

1. Leo Steffens, interview

2. Linda Palisch, interview

3. *Republic Monitor,* September 30, 1975

Chapter 23
RIDGE STORIES

Courtesy of Martin Stueve Family

Over the course of almost eighty years I have been told Ridge stories. A couple I experienced myself. Some of the stories are worth telling because they reflect the times of those past years. In the following I will recall these stories.

The Knocked-Out Goose

My grandfather was blessed with a passel of grand-daughters. There were Nancy, Marcia, Mary, Barbara and Carolyn. These girls were also about the same age with Carolyn being the oldest and "wisest". When the occasion arose that they were back on the Ridge on the same day, there was bound to be trouble. Together the four younger girls explored the entire farm and all the buildings. Grandma was happy when they were exploring and not bothering her in the kitchen.

One such afternoon the girls were playing and exploring near the chicken house. Grandma had a flock of about six geese. Or as Barbara called them "gooses". There was one that was particularly mean. It would chase and if you turned your back, it was known to attack your legs or rear end. This particular day, it threatened the girls. Another little older cousin, Carolyn was there to help. She picked up a pear and threw it at the goose. She hit it in the head and it fell. She and the girls thought it was dead. Now what to do? Grandma will *Schimpfen* (scold) if she finds out we killed her goose.

A plan was hatched. Take the goose to the barn and hide it under some hay. By the time the goose is found we will be long gone. The goose was hidden.

That same evening the uncles were milking and grandpa was forking hay down from the loft for the horses. The goose woke up. With much to say the goose came out of the hay. Grandpa could not believe what he saw. He got the goose out of the barn and finished his work. All the while he thought the girls must have been involved somehow. He waited until everyone was seated at the table for supper.

The parents all listened without a clue. Then grandpa looked at the girls and asked if they knew anything about the goose. They could not keep a secret. Then Carolyn admitted to the crime and the rest of the girls admitted to helping cover-up the crime. It was the first "Ridge Gate". The parents had a good laugh with grandpa issuing a stern warning that the next time you are guilty of something similar to this, confess what you did.

Sleeping on a Corn Husk Mattress

I probably was no more that five or six years old. Mom and dad were staying overnight on the farm. It got late and it was time for me to go to bed. I asked where I would sleep. Grandma said she made a bed for me upstairs on the floor. She said that she got an old mattress out of an upstairs closet.

I went up to find my bed. I undressed and climbed in. It sounded "crunchy" but it was comfortable. I spent the night sleeping on a cornhusk mattress. How many of the readers of this book have slept on a corn husk mattress?

Bugs on New Year's Eve

I probably was no more than five or six years old. Mom and dad were staying overnight on the Ridge. Four husbands were involved in this New Year's Eve event plus their wives, Norbert and Harry my mom's brothers, Elsie mom's sister, Norbert's wife Dorothy and Harry's wife Lorene and Elsie's husband Norris, plus my father. Of course, the children stayed with grandma. Eight folks loaded into one car and headed for an end of the year dance. The destination was Hank's Park near Shawneetown on highway 61. After a night of revelry and about one o'clock in the morning, the group started back to the Ridge. It was raining rather hard. They eventually came to the bottom of the steep Ridge hill. My dad got a lot of advice about what gear to put the car in and how fast to drive. You see the hill was steep, it was raining and the road was muddy. Add to this, all the men had drunk all the liquor they needed.

The group started up the hill. At about half way the car started to slow down. The car was "fishtailing" and getting dangerously close the road ditch. Finally, it happened! They were in the ditch. The men said they could push the car back on the road. No luck! Now what to do?

Two men walked up the hill to Edmund Weber's home. No lights were on. They knocked. In just a bit, Edmund came to the door. He agreed to help. It was decided they would walk to Otto Weber's farm next to Edmund's home. There they would borrow a team of horses and go pull the car out of the ditch. This they did.

The car was pulled to the top of the hill. All went well. Dad said the women got to ride up the hill while he steered the car. Edmund said he would drive them home in his truck. The roads were just too muddy for a car. It was one mile to the house. Edmund got the truck out of a shed. It was old with no front fenders.

The four ladies got in the cab of the truck with Edmund. The men stood on the running boards. They no more than started down the road when the men stared complaining about the bugs. They were all swatting bugs. The bugs seemingly appeared in the middle of the winter on New Year's Eve. The trip only took minutes.

At the house, the four men were able to identify the bugs. Without fenders the tires of the truck were throwing up mud. The four men were covered with mud.

Grandma heard the commotion and came out in her robe. She informed the men that they were not coming into the house the way they were. The ladies brought the summer kitchen water. One went and found a five-gallon bucket. The washing began while the ladies found clean clothes. They left and allowed the men to put their clothes on.

And so, it was that bugs invaded the Ridge on New Year's Eve.

Lightening Hits the Walnut Tree

I was staying on the farm for a week. It was toward evening. Grandpa and I were starting to feed the hogs. A thunderstorm was approaching. Grandpa said that we had best hurry. He dispatched me to get a five-gallon bucket from the barn.

I did as I was instructed. On my way back to the hog pen, a bolt of lightening struck the walnut tree at the foot of the hill next to the pond. It scared me. I dropped the bucket and just stood still. I was frozen in place. Grandpa came around the corner. "What was that?" I pointed at the walnut tree. It was destroyed. "Are you ok?" grandpa asked. I said, "I'm scared!".

That is as close to a lightening strike as I ever want to be.

The Mocking Bird

We all know what a mocking bird is. The bird can emulate the sound or song of another bird. Hence the name "mocking".

Grandma had a favorite mocking bird. It always sat in the cherry tree at the far end of the garden.

My dad decided to do a little rifle practice. My job was to run to a distant spot and hang up a target. While we were doing this the mocking bird decided to serenade us. Dad decided to shoot the mocking bird. With good aim he fired. He missed! Again, he missed! Grandma saw what was going on. Here she came. Dad got *schimpfen* (scolding). That bird was her favorite and how dare dad tries to kill it.

After grandma left, dad said, "boy am I glad I missed! What would she have said if I would have hit the bird."

Norbert Exits the Outhouse

The outhouse was short distance from the house. The door was generally open unless someone was inside. Uncle Norbert needed to use the facility. He was in a hurry. His overalls were beginning to come down as he entered. He did not notice but a goose was laying on the floor in the corner. Norbert sat down and the goose got up. The goose didn't want any company. All kinds of hell broke loose. Here came Norbert out with his overalls barely up. Remember the girls? They saw the whole thing and had quite a laugh watching a grown man run from a goose.

Think it might be the same goose that ended up in the hayloft?

Harry's Dead

Grandpa decided the fields needed lime. A lime crusher was in the area and for a fee the owner would crush your limestone rock. On the back end of the farm was a "flat-rock" creek. Here was all the limestone you needed.

Harry and Norbert carried all the small limestone rocks and piled them. The two men even took a wagon to the end of their property and hauled the smaller rocks to the pile.

Now came the hard part. They would use a sledge hammer and chisel to break large rocks. One would hold the chisel while the other swung the sledge hammer. All was going well. Then a missed swing of the sledge hammer by Norbert.

The sledge hammer glanced off the chisel and caught Harry on the side of the head. Harry was knocked out. Norbert ran to the house. He saw grandpa and said, "Harry's dead!"

Grandpa called grandma and the three ran to the site. When they got there Harry was sitting up and wondering what happened to Norbert. One can only imagine the relief.

The Straw Hat

In 1947, we were visiting the Ridge. It was the Fourth of July. My dad had purchased for me a sack of fireworks. In the sack was a dozen large firecrackers. I remember them to be about one and a half inches long and red. After firing one I had an idea. I found an empty tin can. I lit the fire cracker and put the can over it. The can blew about twenty feet into the air.

Sitting under the shade of the apple tree in the front yard were my dad, grandpa and my two uncles. They applauded my feat. I followed up with another "rocket launch". I did this until I had one left.

In the yard laying next to dad was his brand-new Sunday straw hat. Why not launch his hat up into the air? I simply picked up the hat unnoticed and walked away about fifteen feet. I lit the firecracker, put the hat on top if it and calmly stepped back. The result was not what I expected. The hat stayed on the ground. But I blew the entire top out of the hat. Bits of the hat scattered the yard. I was scared of dad and the rest of the men. I today can still hear dad yell "CHARLIE"! I froze. The rest of this tale you can imagine. That ended fireworks…forever.

A little side note about fireworks!

However, Uncle Harry also loved fireworks, in particular cherry bombs. You all know how loud those can be. One evening returning from the Ridge, Uncle Harry, Aunt Lorene and Nancy, my mom and dad and Barbara were in the same car. Dad was driving. Uncle Harry (much to Aunt Lorene's chagrin) pulled out a cherry bomb. Using his cigar, he little the bomb. As dad drove across Apple Creek bridge Harry intended to through it out the car window onto the bridge. He missed. The cherry bomb fell to the floorboard and scared the life out of everyone when it exploded. Then Harry got a *schimpfen* (scolding) from Aunt Lorene!

SOURCES

1. Barbara Rauh Powell

2. Personal experiences

Chapter 24
CHARIVARI
(Shivaree and Housewarming)

Photo Courtesy of Martin Stueve Family

On the Ridge it was not all work and no play. People got together for special events. Families got together for a confirmation dinner to honor a newly confirmed member of the family. There were baptisms, dances in a new barn or shed and of course there were weddings. Often the whole community was invited. After a young couple were married, that occasion for a housewarming. When these events took place, there was always food and music.

On the Ridge, you looked forward to a *Charivari* or *Shivaree.* From here on, we will use the spelling Shivaree. The Germans living on the Ridge in that day or now know no French. The word charivari is a French word. Webster defines it as "a mock serenade of dissonant noise done with kettles and tin horns meant to annoy."

Shivaree began in in Europe. They spread to England. Different countries had their own unique ways of doing a Shivaree. We will confine our description of such an event to the celebrations on the Ridge.

A Shivaree took place after a couple were married. During the early years, a wedding reception was held at the home of either the bride or the groom. Generally, this took place at the groom's home. There was a limited amount of space available and as a result, not everyone was invited. The guest list was limited to family.

Friends of the bride and groom would want to celebrate the marriage. A Shivaree was planned. It all started after the wedding guests had enjoyed a meal and wedding gifts opened. Then came the Shivaree folks. They were generally the young friends of the bride and groom and had not been invited to the wedding.

The group would pull up in cars. They got out with their noise makers. They would ring cowbells, beat on pots and pans, rattle a gunny sack full of tin cans. They made as much noise as possible. The bride and groom would invite their friends in the yard to enjoy a beer or two or three or four. If there was leftover food they also ate. It was quite a celebration. When everyone was sufficiently inebriated, the folks left.

I know of an instance when the bride and groom were forced to dance in a hog trough brought into the yard. Someone would offer a wedding toast. Fun was had by all.

There was yet more fun to be had. Everyone enjoyed a housewarming. When a young couple moved into their first home their friends had another reason for a party. The house warming was a bit more sinister. Friends of a young couple planned an evening to pay a visit to the first home of the bride and groom. They often brought gifts to adorn the home. Sometimes they chipped in and depending on the amount of money, a very nice gift was purchased.

On the evening of the housewarming, the folks showed up at the house and parked a distance away to avoid being noticed. They waited until the lights went out. After they thought the coupled were comfortably settled, here they came! Often noise makers were again used. One can only imagine the reaction of the married couple. My sister recalls attending a Shivaree about 1955. The couple's lights went out and our dad and his brother "shot an anvil" to let the couple know the revelers were there. To shoot an anvil, one "loads" it with gun powder and a wick. The wick is lit and the noise is like a cannon going off. The problem with shooting off an anvil is that it goes straight up off the ground and one never knows for certain where it will land. The anvil on this occasion was located in dad's brother's field so it wouldn't hit the house or the revelers. That was quite an experience.

By the beginning of the housewarming, it was already late in the evening. The revelers had already drunk quite a lot of beer. For this reason, a housewarming usually took place on Friday or

Saturday evening. I recall attending a house warming when I was young (1940's). The group took their own music with them for a dance. The band was Adde and Reinhold Jungclaus. Adde played the accordion and Reinhold played the guitar. These two played for many dances on the Ridge. The furniture in the living room was pushed aside. Cornmeal was spread on the floor to make the floor slick. Let the fun begin!

So, it was on the Ridge. They worked hard and they played hard.

SOURCES

1. Interview, Girard Fiehler

2. Interview, John Rauh

3. Wikipedia, Charviari

Chapter 25
EDMUND WEBER
And
WEBER'S STORE AND TAVERN

Edmund Weber grew up on the Ridge as the son of a farmer. His father, Otto farmed his ground for many years. His two sons, Leo and Edmund helped with the farm work. During the intervening years Edmund worked away from home at various jobs. The time came for Edmund to decide about the rest of his life. Would it be farming and perhaps jobs as he could find them or would it possibly be something else?

Edmund surveyed his situation in life. The Weber's owned ground at a crossroads on the Ridge. To the east lay Wittenberg about five miles. To the west was Steffens Orchard. The road to the north took you to Star Landing. The road south went to Altenburg. It was five miles to Altenburg. Edmund Weber saw the need for a community store to serve the area residents. After all, gas was 20¢ a gallon and you traveled on re-cap tires. At that time in history five miles on a gravel road was a long distance. There were about thirty families living within two miles of the Ridge.

Edmund was a visionary. He saw a need and with his location, it seemed a perfect place to open a store. The Ridge people would not have to travel all the way to Fischer's store to purchase groceries. There was another ingredient to throw into the mix. The Ridge School was on one corner of the crossroads. Every day during the school year, parents brought the children to school. This would serve as a major draw to a store.

Edmund Weber did not just open a store. This was a planned adventure with a vision and a dream. The first store building was put into use. Later this building would be used as a place for Edmund to sell feed. One can only imagine the anxious moments Edmund had when he opened his new business. The year was 1938 and a new business was about to open.

The dream worked. The business was a success. It was so much a success, that in 1946 Edmund decided to build a new store building. The building was constructed so that one half of the building was a grocery store and the other half a tavern. Over the years the business had several names which the people gave it. It was called *Weber's Place, The Ridge Tavern, Weber's Tavern, Weber's Tavern and Grocery Store, Edmund's place and The Place on the Ridge.*

Weber's Place became the focal point on the Ridge. Everything centered on activity at Edmund's. The National Farmers Organization held their meetings in the store. If there was a birthday to celebrate, the tavern was the perfect place. Edmund bought the first television on the Ridge. On Saturday night everyone gathered to watch the wrestling and boxing matches. Watching these matches were almost as important as church on Sunday.

The first known settler on the Ridge, seems to have been Theodore Holschen. He came to America in 1839. He came the same year the Saxons led by Martin Stephan immigrated. Theodore Holschen met the Saxons. He himself was from Hanover, Germany. It is believed he traveled to Perry County with the Saxon group. He purchased his land on the Ridge, forty acres, for $1.46 per acre. The land was just north of Weber's Place. When all the early settlers had arrived, the Altenburg Saxons located themselves near Seelitz, Dresden, Altenburg and Frohna. The folks on the Ridge all came from Hanover, Saxony.

Initially the Ridge was called *Friedland*. This translates from the German as *"land of peace"*. Never was a town established here. In 1898 The area had a mailing address. The postal route ran from Wittenberg to Appleton. The mailing address was Star Route No. 45755.

Edmund Weber saw another opportunity. The area needed a blacksmith shop. A blacksmith shop opened. Over the years it was in business, Marvin Lorenz and Patrick Hughey were the blacksmiths. Edmund Weber bought cream from area farmers and sold it to a local creamery. If a farmer had a flat tire, you could get it fixed at Edmund's. There were two Texaco gas pumps. Now you did not have to drive to Fiehler's Garage where you pumped Phillips 66. Edmund was known to call square dances. He had pool tournaments and he sold Knap shoes.

Edmund Weber was always looking for a business opportunity. Farmers would purchase baby chicks to use for laying hens. There were special Vantress Roosters for the flock. You brought the eggs to Edmund who in turn shipped them to a hatchery. The result would be fryers for super-markets.

Edmund Weber is far from finished in expanding his business. People of the Ridge had to travel to Altenburg for a haircut. That was business that could remain on the Ridge. Edmund attended a barber school in St. Louis. If you wanted to look good at church for 25¢ you could get your hair cut. I understand even the girls could get a haircut from Edmund! Marcia Stueve says she had haircuts from Edmund.

Next came a visionary's vision. Would you believe it? Edmund Weber constructed a three-room motel unit. He would rent the rooms to squirrel hunters and to fisherman. There were two fishing ponds just behind the store. Edmund would advertise fishing tournaments. He drew crowds. If you left a crack in the door Edmund would walk through and expand his business.

We should not forget Edmund's wife, Verna. She worked hard and supported Edmund in all that he was doing. Not only was she involved in the business she also raised four children: Arlene, Ruby, Mary and Richard. When they came into the store they mainly got in the way and were quickly dispatched to the house next door. Arlene, as the oldest, did work at the store. Richard became the official flat tire fixer, worm digger for the fisherman and anything else his father could find to keep him busy. The youngest, Mary, remembers going into the store and eating candy. Her dad would catch her and remind Mary that she eating up the profit.

Whenever I get into conversation about the Ridge, the subject of shooting matches at the Weber's Place comes up. Especially, they want to talk about the matches before Thanksgiving and Christmas when the winners could select live turkeys, geese and ducks. The folks came from miles around to shoot in these matches. Without a doubt, Edmund's Thanksgiving or Christmas matches were the largest in all of Perry County. I left a match one day with a live turkey in the trunk of my car. Imagine what my trunk was like when I got home.

I recall as a little boy driving to the Ridge to visit my grandparents. My dad always had a cigar in his mouth. One particular day we were at the bottom of the steep hill which ascended to the top of the Ridge and Weber's Place. I said, *"dad, I'm sick. Could I get a lemon soda at Weber's?"* Dad stopped at Edmund's and I got my soda. From that time on, I feigned a sick stomach whenever we came to the bottom of the Ridge hill. It worked about half of the time. My younger siblings kept this "tradition" up and they had success on occasion.

Weber's store closed in 1964. With the closing, a wonderful chapter in Ridge history closed with it. Edmund Weber and his store were, for two decades the focal point of the Ridge. A man born on the Ridge saw a community need and he set out to meet that need. Whatever the Ridge needed, Edmund saw to it. He sold groceries and beer, Texaco gas, haircuts and hatching eggs and on and on. Edmund wanted to be a service to the community. He was a husband, father and Christian gentleman. He was a visionary. He could see a need and the future if that need was met. Thanks Edmund for the community servant you were. Perhaps the chapter in Ridge history will keep your memory alive.

SOURCES

1. Interview, Richard Weber and Mary Weber Kiehne

Chapter 26
THE RIDGE CLUB

The men on the Ridge and surrounding area worked hard. All was not work. These men had fun and had a good time in associating with each other. As time lapsed, it became easier to travel. Roads were better and cars were available. The men formed a club for the purpose of fellowship and entertainment.

There exists a minute book kept by various members of the club. The first secretary was Edmund Weber. Two of his children, Richard Weber and Mary Weber Kiehne allowed me the privilege of reading the minutes kept. The minutes conclude in 1963. It is a bit difficult to determine the exact date the club was formed. In this chapter the minutes will be summarized. Not all the minutes will be included.

The official name of the club was The Ridge Community Club. The first minutes were recorded in April with no year date. At this meeting the first officers were elected:

Edgar Leimbach	President
Edmund Weber	Vice-President
Leo Steffens	Secretary-Treasure

A set of rules and regulations was the first order of business. These are as follows:

1. It was decided that we would have our business meetings the first Tuesday of each month.

2. It was decided that the membership dues should be $2.50 and the monthly dues be 50¢.
3. A person must be 16 years of age to be eligible to join the club.
4. The club will vote on it if any person want to join this club. 2/3 majority will rule.
5. There will be no gambling allowed in this hall. Note: the Hall is The Ridge School building.
6. Majority will rule in all business meetings except when voting on new members.
7. If any person that doesn't belong to the club want to attend Club socials he will have to be invited by a club member.
8. Herbert Steffens, Willard Schroeder, Norbert Stueve were Elected ushers. Note: it is interpreted that these ushers were the "bouncers."

The minute book next has six (6) years of records of who paid their dues by each month. It is at this point we have year dates appearing. Counting back, it appears the club was formed in 1951 during the month of April.

The first members of the club were:

Edmund Weber	Arnold Leimbach
Edgar Leimbach	Leo Steffens
Leo Weber	Elton Weber
Erhard Gerler	Norman Weber
Herbert Steffens	Ellis Leimbach
Floyd Steffens	Arthur Jungclaus
Larry Steffens	Otto Wichern

Leonard Wichern	Willard Schroeder
Edgar Hecht	Willard Schattauer
Clarence Piltz	Norbert Stueve
Eugene Hecht	

Next, we find in the minute book listing of club expenses for the year 1951. Following, I have selected a few items for the listing:

Piano Tuning	$10.00
Broom	1.00
After meeting social	3.40
(that would be beer)	
Tables and chairs	31.42
Dart Ball Board	4.00
Fish and Lard	32.79
Joe Schroeder-electricity	4.00
(they tapped his line for electricity)	
Weber for cardboard and fish	13.20

Minutes – April 1951

Decided to have a fish fry in May. Edmund Weber to get 50 pounds of jack salmon.
Edmund will also get a half barrel of beer. A non-member can rent the hall for $5.00

Minutes – June 1951

Decided the members would divide the left-over fish from the fish fry. Decided to buy a screen door for the building.

Minutes – August 1951

It was decided that a person attending a dance would be charged 35¢ if he was not a member.

Minutes – December 1951

Decided that Eugene Hecht be taken in as a new member.

Minutes – January 1952

Edgar Leimbach elected to be the new President.
Edmund Weber elected Vice-President
Edgar Hecht elected Secretary-Treasure

Minutes - February 1952

There were only eight members present. We didn't have much of a meeting.

Minutes – June 1952

A motion was made to have a fish fry on the tenth of June.

Minutes – September 1952

It was decided that we join the Dart Ball Club if we can get into it. Clarence Piltz was elected captain of our dart ball team. We decided to have some practice games.

Minutes – October 1952

It was decided to buy a dozen darts.

Minutes - January 1953

We elected new officers. They are:

Herbert Steffens	President
Edmund Weber	Vice-President
Edgar Hecht	Secretary-Treasure
Clarence Piltz	Dart Ball Captain

The minutes of the club are recorded for every month. It seems that fish fries, socials, dances and dart ball were the main activities. It is interesting to note the club never had their own electric service. They continue to use the Joe Schrader electric services and paid him a monthly fee of $1.50. The expense items show many checks to Edmund Weber for drinks and fish. Never do the minutes say "beer". The income for the club averages near $100.00 month. In 1954 the club held their first "chicken fry." There is an entry for income received from "fishing rodeo picnic dinner." The amount was $35.00. No mention of this in the minutes.

There is mention in 1957 of a benefit dance for tornado relief of Eldor Weber and Leo Steffens. The minutes of the club continue until May 1963. During that year there is no mention of disbanding the club. Perhaps there is a minute book that continues the activity of this group?

The men on the Ridge needed and wanted a detraction from the daily routine of farming fellowship with each other was important to these folks. They came together and for many years enjoyed fish fries and dances. The ladies would get involved

155

providing food for parties. What is important to note is that they identified themselves as a community set apart. There was a need for social life and they filled that need. We tip our hats the Ridge Club.

SOURCES

1. Richard Weber, Minute Book by Edmund Weber

Chapter 27
THE RIDGE BAND

The Ridge Club certainly added to the social life of the community. There was a need that needed to be filled. There was another group founded earlier than the Ridge Club. It was the Ridge Band. The only thing we know about that group is a picture that exists today. The picture indicated the band was in existence in the 1920's.

This band should not be confused with the Altenburg Band. That band came later and a different group of men. The Ridge Band had twelve members. Twelve men could certainly make a lot of noise and I'll bet some good music. If you know of or have any information about this group please give it to the Lutheran Heritage Center and Museum in Altenburg, Missouri.

The members of the band are:

(front, from the left)

Gerhardt Thurm, Herman Leimbach, Herman Gerler, Henry Leimbach, Joe Jungclaus

(back, from the left)

Ludwig Gerler, Joe Seibel, Ernst Leimbach, C. Palisch, Emanuel Weber, Emanuel Stueve and August Leimbach

Perry County Album

Ridge Band - Circa 1920

o Steffens of Frohna submitted this photo of the Ridge Band that played in the 1920's "on the ridge" in East Perry County, ac
; to Steffens. The members are (front, from left) Gerhardt Thurm, Herman Leimbach, Herman Gerler, Henry Leimbach,
gdaus. Back—Ludwig Gerler, Joe Seibel, Ernst Leimbach, C. Pallsch, Emanuel Weber, Emanuel Stueve, and August Leimbac
'ry County Republic-Monitor invites readers to submit photographs of general historical significance for publication in this a
otos will be returned unharmed and may be picked up at the newspaper office after publication.

Courtesy of the *Perry County Republic Monitor*

Chapter 28
GEMEINDE – KIRCHE - KAMRADSCHAFT – ARBEIT UND GEMULICHKEIT

The five German words identifying this chapter certainly describe life on the Ridge. These words translate into the English language as *community, church, fellowship, work and friendship.*

If there is one word that describes life in the early years of the Ridge it is *Gemeinde,* or community. These folks very early called the *Gemeinde*, Friedland. There never was an established or registered town called Friedland. The designation for the area soon changed to the Ridge. The Ridge was a *Gemeinde* from the beginning and remains that way today.

A *Gemeinde* is a group of people living together and having the same interests, the same work, and having these in common. The same interests are evident when we look back at the early history of these German settlers. Early on, survival was a common interest. They left their homeland and were never to return. They simply had to make this immigration work. They had to have food and shelter. The result was they all had this in common and they worked together in order that the *Gemeinde* would survive.

Think about this! You wake up in the morning and know that in three months it will turn cold and snow. I must build a house to live in. Your neighbor across the field is faced with the same challenge. You have a mutual interest and you help each other in meeting the challenge.

When your house was built the mutual interests changed. Now you must earn a living farming. This was now to the folks from Hanover. They had not farmed before. These folks were linen weavers and cobblers. The settler and his neighbor learned together. This took place all along the Ridge.

This sense of *Gemeinde* never left the Ridge. From 1850 until present if your neighbor needed help, then by golly I'll help. That is how these folks survived. They did it by being *Gemeinde*. The problems and challenges you faced, your neighbor faces them also. So, let's get to work.

Gemeinde is such an all-encompassing word. How does one put his arms around this word in order to understand it? The best way to become a part of a *Gemeinde*. Perhaps it is living in a small town. Maybe it is the people at your church. If you live in a large city it might be the street you live on. If in life you have surrounded yourself with people with whom all of you share mutual interest then you know what *Gemeinde* is.

In the case of the Ridge *Gemeinde* was the glue that held all this together was *Kirche*. *Kirche* or church. The Ridge settlers left Hanover as Lutherans. They knew before they left Hanover that a large settlement of Lutherans was already in Perry County.

The early settlers on the Ridge were members of Trinity *Kirche* in Altenburg. In 1857, there was a division of members due to the Schiefferdecker controversy. Immanuel Lutheran *Kirche* was formed the same year with members following Pastor

Schiefferdecker. There were members of the new *Kirche* that lived on the Ridge. It was but a short period of time and Immanuel *Kirche* opened a new parochial school on the Ridge. The pastor of Immanuel *Kirche* that was known to teach school. Because of the school, the folks on the Ridge developed an allegiance to Immanuel *Kirche*.

Immigrants from Germany brought with them a Christian faith. They realized that faith and lived it out each day. You did not live on the Ridge and not go to *Kirche*. The hard working, hardy, ruddy, tough people said their prayers before every meal and before bedtime. They read from their Bible daily.

It was six miles to church in your buggy. Rain or shine you went to *Kirche*. Immanuel *Kirche* saw a need to hold worship services on the Ridge. So, services on Sunday afternoons in the Ridge School came about.

Have you got the picture? Jesus Christ was the center of their lives.

Kamradschaft is fellowship. This is a mutual sharing of interests. It is brother-ship. When you are two thousand miles from home, you cannot live on an island. You have to all share with each other. You care about each other. These immigrants needed to be cared for and they needed to care for each other. This was the life of the Ridge settlers.

How do you demonstrate care when you live a mile from your neighbor? You visit! On Friday or Saturday evening, you loaded the family in the buggy or wagon and you drove to a neighbor for a visit. This was an unannounced visit. Before you left home, mom baked a coffee cake or a large cake.

The folks with whom you were visiting saw you coming. Quickly the house was picked up and the front porch readied. A pot of coffee was started on the kitchen wood stove.

The men sat on the front porch and "talked." The women were jabbering in the kitchen with the children playing. One needs to remember that this "visit" was a major event. The men talked about many things. They talked about when the Civil War might end. Also, they talked about Pastor's sermon last Sunday. They talked about the crops and the weather. The women talked about their garden and canning vegetables. They talked about new clothes for their children.

After the conversation ran out, out came the cake and coffee. The time went by quickly. This was Kamradshaft. In about a month the "visit" would be repaid.

The men in the *gemeitude* needed *Kamradschaft*. In a previous chapter you read about the Ridge Social Club that was formed. They fried and ate fish, played darts and they danced to lively music. Back then you had to learn how to waltz, do the two-step and dance a polka.

There was *Arbeit*. Work! Many chapters in the account of the Ridge describes the hard *Arbeit*. Today we are accustomed to an eight-hour day of work. Then it was before day light until after dark. You ate breakfast to the light of a kerosene lamp and you ate supper likewise. The days were long and the sun was just as hot as it is today, it was just as cold as it is today and there was more work than could be completed in a day.

These Germans put their shoulders to the wheel and kept them there. Their hands were on the handles of a plow until they bled. They did the *Arbeit* we do today but our hands don't have to bleed today. These were remarkable folks. Remember this, the wives and children worked just as hard. There was plenty *Arbeit* to go around.

Finally, there was *Gemütlichkeit.* This is a different word to translate into the English. In fact, I'm told that it cannot be translated into an English word. That is because it is a feeling. It is a word that describes a feeling among a group of people. It encompasses fellowship, friendship, high regard and a number of other similar adjectives. *Gemütlichkeit* is the warm happy feeling you have when you are among a group of people.

Gemütlichkeit is certainly appropriate in describing the community on the Ridge. There was a special feeling they had for each other. The Ridge folks were an isolated community They were six miles from Altenburg. That doesn't say much today. Today one can get in his car and in a few minutes, you can purchase groceries in Altenburg. In 1900 the trip to Altenburg was lengthy. The people had to stay together and relate to each other. *Gemütlichkeit* enveloped. There was a special feeling between the Ridge folks.

It was *gememud, Kirche, Kamradschaft, Arbeit* and *Gemutlichkeit.* There is nothing wrong with these five. These words are vital descriptive words. If there is to be a community. Without these words you do not have a community. This is the Ridge.

Chapter 29
THE FINAL FIVE

We have established that the Ridge was a community not a town. The community originally gave themselves the name Friedland. This Land of Peace or Peaceful Land encompassed a large area. Perhaps as much as seven miles by three miles. This area could be stretched to include an even larger area if one included the people and farms half way to Altenburg

These were church going Lutherans. They did not hide their faith but publicly demonstrated a resolve that the God of this universe could see them through any adversity, be that illness, accidents, death, tornados or any other happening in their lives. When one looks back to the time and circumstances in which these hearty folks began life in the United States, we can say nothing else but well done.

The Ridge folks began with very little. They literally grubbed out an existence with grubbing hoes and an axe. They began their day clearing the land. When the trees were removed and fields appeared, the fields were hills. If the immigration was to work they would need to adapt to hill-farming. They were not deterred. If the field was too steep to plant crops then it became a hayfield and pasture ground. On the Ridge, you need not worry about floods, you only hoped your cows would not fall out of a field.

Initially these farmers used very crude implements to farm their farms. There was no mower to mow hay, you used a mowing scythe. Without a hay-baler you hauled your hay to the barn

164

loose. Corn was plowed with a single row plow or a double-shovel. Grain at first was not threshed but flailed. Later came the binder and the threshing machine. The ladies made soap, apple butter and washed clothes on a washboard. They worked just as hard as the men. It was difficult in the beginning for Ridge people.

Slowly, ever so slowly, things got better. Along came the tractor and the automobile. At first only the most prosperous could afford these. Then wonder of wonders there came electric lines to the Ridge. Finally came the day when mom got rid of her wood cooking stove and she got a brand-new kerosene stove. Now that was as good as it gets. And one more thing, the kids walked to school, uphill both ways!

Such were the beginning on the Ridge. There is so much more that could be written. Everyone who experienced life on the Ridge had their own story to tell. Tell you stories to your kids and grandkids. The story needs never to be lost or forgotten. Perhaps this book will help keep the story alive. Let us all continue to tell the Ridge story. This story is about real people. They were real people determined to survive in a new country. These folks gave us a wonderful heritage.

A heritage is something handed down by our ancestors. Our ancestors from the Ridge handed us a heritage that gave us an example of courage. Courage enough to leave Germany and seek a better life. They said good-bye to a former life, traveled into the unknown to begin a life that would be better for them, their children and the generations to follow.

These Christian people gave us an example of a work ethic. Just how hard can you work? Can you handle sun-up till after dark? Can you swing an axe until your hands bleed? Can you do that every day? That's what they did!

There is so much handed down to us. The most important is a knowledge of Jesus Christ. God's word is our greatest heritage. Our ancestors would not lay that down or put it aside. It was center in all they did. I can still see my Grandfather sitting at the kitchen table reading his Bible to the light of the kerosene lantern.

The history of the Ridge has given us much to contemplate. An interesting question is who of all the settlers and early folks on the Ridge stand out as men who distinguished themselves above others. It is risky to identify those, others, rose above others as businessmen and successful men in the Ridge area. I have decided to take the risk. The people I will name are ranked in no special order but these men certainly stand out.

I will begin with Daniel Wichern. He immigrated to the United States seeking a better life as did all the immigrants. After working for another person at a boat landing he began his own landing. He called it Star Landing. He shipped goods to the St. Louis markets and received supplies for local farmers. He opened a mercantile store. If that's not enough, he operated a ferryboat operation in Illinois. He farmed and bought an island in the Mississippi River to farm. Daniel Wichern was a visionary. He saw a need and filled the need.

Next, I choose Rudy Steffens. For a couple of reasons, he is named. Everyone knows of his orchard business. He knew the success of George Hatch at Seventy-Six, why not do the same thing? He bought land and planted fruit trees. Rudy sold his fruit in Soulard in St. Louis, Cape Girardeau, Rozier's Store in Perryville and who can forget the fruit stand in Altenburg? After you attended the East Perry County Fair before you left Altenburg you bought apples at Steffens Fruit Stand.

Another side of Rudy Steffens is his association with the black community at Mack's Chapel. He employed the black community to work in his orchard and day laborers on his farm. All this in a time when white people were not expected to associate with blacks. His family occasionally worked at Mack's Chapel and attended baptisms at Rudy' farm pond.

Let us mention John Wilkinson at Seventy-Six. This little town was just down the hill from the Steffen's Farm. John Wilkinson climbed out of the river after his boat sank and he decided that at this spot he would begin life all over.

He salvaged boards from his sunken boat and built a shanty for a house. He cut cord wood and sold it to river captains. Then he hired men to cut wood. The cord wood business became the largest wood business on the Mississippi River. Next, he built a store for area residents even to the point of a lady's hat shop. As his money increased he took the profits and bought land eventually owning 120,000acres. He was the wealthiest man in Perry County and perhaps the state of Missouri. John Wilkinson stands out.

Edmund Weber became the Ridge barber. For twenty-five cents you could look good at church on Sunday. Then came gas pumps selling Texaco gas. If the community needed something, Edmund handled it.

Edmund Weber and his store-tavern became the focal point of the Ridge He gave the Ridge identity. Everything focused on Edmund and Verna. In between all effort the store required Edmund work on the family farm and he and Verna raised four children.

I have found that a discussion on the Ridge inevitably goes to the shooting matches at Weber's Tavern. All want to talk about the live turkeys, geese and duck matches. Just Before Thanksgiving and Christmas Edmund would advertise the shooting match. The people came from miles around. Imagine the mess in your car if you went home with a live turkey in your trunk. Folks today just don't understand why we call those early days fun.

Edmund Weber emerges as a visionary, businessman, father, community leader and a Christian gentleman. He and Verna are very much a part of Ridge history.

Finally, I must mention Ed Leimbach. He began life from a meager existence. He was forced to work on a farm in Iowa for room and board. That is a meager beginning. He serves as an example of picking yourself up by your own bootstraps. When he returned to Perry County, the world was at war. Ed enlisted for the draft. He was sent to Fort Dodge, Iowa for training.

Perry County has a system of commissioners to help make county decisions. These commissioners today deal mainly with roads and are elected by districts. Ed Leimbach entered the election to represent East Perry County. He was elected. In the earlier years the commissioners were called Judges. Ed was now a county judge. He served many years in this capacity. He was respected enough to be elected Presiding Judge which meant he was chairman of the judges.

From a teenager relegated to work for no compensation, only room and board to Presiding County Judge. He was a successful farmer, father, businessman and church leader. Ed Leimbach emerges as standing apart within his community.

There you have it. Daniel Wichern, John Wilkinson, Rudy Steffens, Edmund Weber and Ed Leimbach. If you disagree then you get to write the next book.

The interesting question being are there any alive today who will emerge as successful farmers on the Ridge? The answer to this question is yes. But no names until they pass away and become history themselves. They are on the Ridge emerging. You get to tell their story when you write the next book.

As long as there are people on the Ridge there will be history. The Ridge isn't going away. When God created the Ridge, he piled up enough limestone rock that it isn't going to leave. Our Lord created that isolated place in order that it be settled and farmed. The folks chosen for the task were from Hanover, Germany. They came and hacked out an existence.

Some say, "settle in that God-forsaken area of Perry County?" It was not forsaken. God was right beside these people because they kept Him there. When they built their barns and cleaned the fence rows, He was there.

If you have ties to the Ridge then you have a heritage of which to be very proud. You are related to *Gemeinde, Kirche, Kamradschaft, Arbeit and Gemutlichkeit.*

Made in the USA
Monee, IL
07 May 2022

96063926R00111